The Post-Modern Presidency

THE
POST-MODERN
PRESIDENCY

The Office
after
Ronald Reagan

RYAN J. BARILLEAUX

PRAEGER

New York
Westport, Connecticut
London

Library of Congress Cataloging-in-Publication Data

Barilleaux, Ryan J.
  The post-modern presidency.

  Bibliography: p.
  Includes index.
  1. Presidents—United States. 2. United States—
Politics and government—1981– . 3. Reagan,
Ronald. I. Title.
JF255.B37   1988   321.8′042′0973   87–25861
ISBN 0–275–92721–0

Library of Congress Catalog Card Number: 87–25861

ISBN: 0–275–92721–0

First published in 1988

Praeger Publishers, One Madison Avenue, New York, NY 10010
A division of Greenwood Press, Inc.

Printed in the United States of America

The paper used in this book complies with the
Permanent Paper Standard issued by the National
Information Standards Organization (Z39.48–1984).

10 9 8 7 6 5 4 3 2 1

For my mother

and the memory of my father

Contents

Acknowledgments

Every large scholarly project is a production involving many people who work toward a common goal. This book has benefited from the gracious help I have received from the people listed below. Without their help, I would still be scribbling away in my office.

I want first to pay tribute to my good friend and former colleague, Z. Anthony Kruszewski. Through his encouragement, inspiration, and example, Tony helped me turn my ideas into a book. He also greatly facilitated the writing of this book by providing me with secretarial help. He is a true gentleman and scholar, and one of the finest people I have known.

Many other people helped me to refine my ideas, sharpen my prose, or at least think twice about what I have written. Robert Webking, Edward Paul Fuchs, David Lanoue, Bruce Buchanan, Sharon Davis Rives, Daniel Paul Franklin, Robert Clinton, Phillip Henderson, Michael Greenberg, Karen Johnson, Neil Siegel, and Nolan J. Argyle— all contributed to my thinking about the contemporary presidency, as did some anonymous reviewers whose comments I have received.

My labor in writing this book was greatly eased by the expert assistance I received from several people. Daniel Laurentano and Kathleen Day provided valuable research assistance. Deborah Pancoast helped with administrative matters. Jill Bonar typed the whole manuscript and put up with my atrocious handwriting. Rene Paul Barilleaux instructed me in the vagaries of contemporary design, which gave me the term "post-modern" I use so frequently in this work.

The whole project would have been impossible without the support of my family. Marilyn, Gerard, and Madeleine Barilleaux kept me going through months when this book claimed most of my attention.

A portion of this research was funded by a grant from the F. B. Cotton Memorial Trust. I sincerely appreciate that help. I also want to thank the staff at Praeger Publishers for making this book a reality.

Everyone mentioned above deserves a share in whatever I have accomplished in this book. Of course, I accept complete responsibility for whatever flaws remain.

The
Post-Modern
Presidency

Introduction

Inauguration Day, 1989: As the new president is about to be sworn in, reflective observers note the distinction of the occasion. Of course, they think of the fact that the office has changed hands peacefully and constitutionally forty-one times, but they also note other points marking the transition. This inauguration is the result of the first presidential election in twenty years that did not feature an incumbent seeking reelection.[1] It is also the first time in almost thirty years that the transition of power will be what most Americans, despite contrary historical evidence, consider a "normal" one. a two-term president is retiring after eight years in office.[2]

The new president's accession is also notable in another important way. Here begins the first post-Reagan presidency, so a question on everyone's mind is what mark Mr. Reagan has made on the office he is leaving. Has he changed the presidency, as he has altered the political agenda of the United States?

Certainly observers sense that the presidency has changed, but it is unclear whether such changes were Mr. Reagan's doing, or are larger than that one man. After the upheavals of the past two decades, in the wake of the Vietnam War, Watergate, the "imperial" and "post-imperial" presidencies of the 1960s and 1970s, and the revival of the presidency under Ronald Reagan, the presidency certainly seems different. But, how is it so?

Such questions are the concern of this book. How has the presidency changed? Why has the presidency changed? Are the apparent changes merely cosmetic, or do they affect the nature and operations of the office?

It is my contention that the contemporary presidency is distinctive. The office occupied by Ronald Reagan and his successors is not merely an extension of the modern presidency created by Franklin Roosevelt, but is sufficiently different to warrant a new label. I choose to refer to it as the "post-modern" presidency.

I use the term "post-modern" in the same sense that architectural critics have applied a similar label to the work of Philip Johnson and other contemporary designers. These architects have not completely abandoned the steel and glass of the ubiquitous International Style, but have altered it sufficiently in such projects as Manhattan's AT&T building to demand a new label for their designs: post-modernism. In the same way, the presidency has been altered. It is a useless form of generalizing to consider the presidency of the late twentieth century merely an extension of what has gone before. It is that, but is also something more: what we have now is not just a continuation of the modern presidency, but a post-modern presidency.

The purpose of this book is to examine the shape and character of the post-modern presidency, where it came from, and where it is likely to be headed. This task will be accomplished by a look at the rise and fall of the modern presidency, fashioned by presidents from Franklin Roosevelt to Richard Nixon, and how the "post-imperial" presidencies of Gerald Ford and Jimmy Carter set the stage for a new presidency. The book will also examine changes in the American political environment that affect the presidency, assess the impact of Ronald Reagan on the office, and consider implications of the post-modern presidency for future officeholders.

Critics of my thesis will respond that there really is no difference between the so-called post-modern presidency and the modern presidency everyone knows. I cannot agree. As my lawyer reminds me, a difference in degree may be as important as a difference in kind. The post-modern presidency exhibits both types of differences from its predecessors: certain of its aspects are qualitatively different from the nature of the modern presidency, while other aspects are quantitatively different. Many of the developments examined in this book began under earlier presidents, but have accelerated or expanded enough in recent years to distinguish the contemporary presidency from its forerunners.

Others will contend that some of the changes I describe are not significant enough to indicate a new phase in the evolution of the presidency. I agree: individually, several of these points are minor amendments to the modern presidency. But the cumulative effects of the changes I examine are significant.

The same is true of the modern presidency's distinction from the traditional presidency. Precedents for and examples of many features of the modern institution can be found as far back as Washington's time, but that does not mean that there had been no change in the office. For example, the aggressive legislative leadership associated with Franklin Roosevelt and Lyndon Johnson had roots in the Washington-Hamilton financial program and Jefferson's legislative initiatives, and certainly in the presidencies of Teddy Roosevelt and Woodrow Wilson. But the modern presidency did not exist until FDR and his successors expanded, consolidated, and institutionalized a number of changes in the presidential office.

In the same way, the post-modern presidency I describe in this book is a result of the cumulative effects of change. Does this mean that the whole is greater than the sum of its parts? To some degree, the answer is yes. On the other hand, as I intend to demonstrate, some of the parts are fairly significant.

This book is not an apology for the Reagan presidency. I make that statement because many critics are likely to interpret it that way. As readers will see, however, I find much to criticize in the Reagan White House. But my argument is more fundamental than praise or criticism of the most recent administration. Rather, I see many developments in the Reagan presidency as the culmination of larger trends, with several innovations that are likely to remain. These trends and innovations have reached a point where the presidency has entered a new phase in its evolution, which I label "post-modern." That change and its consequences, not apologia, is the point of my argument.

One last caveat: the purpose of this book is not to report on new data or unique empirical findings. Rather, my purpose is interpretive and analytical. I am examining patterns and relationships that I think others have overlooked. If my treatment of a particular aspect of the post-modern presidency is sketchy, that is because my purpose is to demonstrate how the whole has been changed by alterations in the parts.

Therefore, as Inauguration Day, 1989, approaches, it is time to take stock of the American presidency. Chapter 1 surveys the shape of the contemporary presidency and advances my central thesis. Chapter 2 examines the rise and fall of the modern presidency, so the reader may assess what has happened to the office. The third chapter puts the post-modern presidency in the context of the new American political environment, which is surprisingly different from the American political scene of only twenty or thirty years ago. Chapters 4–6 examine in greater detail the points made in the first chapter. Finally, the concluding chapter attempts to describe the role of the presidency in late twentieth century American politics.

NOTES

1. For the sake of good prose, Gerald Ford's 1976 bid for the presidency has been subsumed under the term "reelection." Of course, Ford had not been elected to the office, but he was the incumbent.

2. Americans like to think of two-term presidencies as normal, despite the fact that most presidents have not served two full terms. Our myths are about stability, even if our reality has been a continual flux.

1   *A New Presidency?*

Ronald Reagan has altered the political agenda of the United States. He has halted the trend of rapid growth in federal government spending, directed attention toward deregulation and greater control of bureaucracy, increased military spending, affected tax cuts and an overhaul of the federal tax code, presided over the establishment of a long-term deficit problem for the national government, and generally challenged the New Deal-Great Society consensus that had framed American political debate for some forty-odd years. His effect on the political agenda has been characterized as the "new direction in American politics" and the "Reagan experiment,"[1] and can be seen most acutely in the changes he has induced in the opposition party.

The Democrats now reflect the changing agenda of American politics. With the single exception of calling for a tax increase, Walter Mondale's 1984 presidential platform consisted largely of an appeal for more "fairness" in the application of Reaganism.[2] In 1986, the Democratic Party issued a report on the future of the party that one disgruntled Democratic activist branded as "me-tooism" of Republican themes.[3] In a number of congressional races that year, successful Democratic candidates were careful to portray themselves as "centrists" and to echo Mr. Reagan's theme of the limits of government. Finally, in the unfolding contest for the 1988 Democratic presidential nomination, the terms of debate continue to reflect the "new direction" inaugurated by Mr. Reagan. While the party has not adopted Mr. Reagan's positions on the questions of public policy, it is fair to say that the issues discussed in the contemporary political debate bear his stamp. Even in the wake of the Iran-Contra affair, the shape of American politics after Mr. Reagan is different than it was before.

But what of the office Mr. Reagan has held? How has it been changed by his tenure?

The institution of the presidency has been changed, but not by Mr. Reagan alone. Rather, it has been affected by him and forces beyond him. The presidency of the late twentieth century is different from the office of only two or three decades ago,[4] but its differences cannot be captured in pithy adjectives such as "stronger," "weaker," or even just "different." An important part of the story is that the changes in the presidency over the last several years are complex and do not all complement one another.

The changes that have occurred in the presidency are diverse. Mr. Reagan has contributed to them by halting the decline of presidential power that marked the decade of the 1970s, and which many observers thought at that time was irreversible.[5] There is now little talk of an "impossible presidency" such as was common under Presidents Ford and Carter, when even senior presidential advisors were suggesting the need for constitutional changes to save the presidency.[6] It is no longer the "fire hydrant of the nation," as then-Vice-President Mondale called it in 1980.[7] Once more, it occupies a position of respect and a potential for leadership.

Mr. Reagan has centralized control of the executive branch in the White House, thus moving toward an "administrative presidency."[8] He has increased presidential control over the executive budget process, government regulation, and the use of military force. In general, he has revived the prerogative powers of the presidency, although often in a different form than they existed before.

Other apparent changes in the presidency reflect trends larger than those that have developed under Mr. Reagan. The Executive Office of the President has been changing for a number of years, so it is larger, more complex, and plays a different role in government than it did only twenty years ago. Mr. Reagan, following his recent predecessors, has put greater emphasis on public appeals for support to influence Congress than did earlier modern presidents. Presidential appointments to judicial

al Science Review
V 83 — S'89 — p1011

)'88 — p711
Studies Quarterly

V 19 — summer 89 — p656

Science Quarterly
Science Quarterly
V104 — summer89 — p339

1946 1986 American po

Bound→choice
V 26

Presiden-

Bound→political

er/ +376

rately

(165(2)
ademy of

, Barilleaux
ice After

Magazine Index +

.R54
1991
Q

and regulatory positions now have a greater impact on the shape of business and social policy. In short, many characteristics of the presidency associated with Ronald Reagan had their origins in earlier administrations.

These long-term trends and Mr. Reagan's own contributions have altered the presidency in a significant way. The new shape of the presidency is "post-modern." It is the modern presidency with a number of adjustments. Ronald Reagan is the first post-modern president, but not because he alone created that position. Rather, he consolidated changes that have been building for years, added his own innovations, and the result is a revised presidential institution. After he leaves Washington, Ronald Reagan's successors will occupy an office that is substantively different from the job John Kennedy and Richard Nixon assumed in their own times.

It's not easy to make out the shape of the post-modern presidency, however, because of the incumbent. There's the rub. Because the office of the presidency is always influenced by the personality of the officeholder, it is difficult to separate the two. But it is not impossible. The post-modern presidency is more than just the long shadow of Mr. Reagan, for as I have said it is a creature of more than his tenure. His personal skills, idiosyncracies, talents, and peccadillos must be excised in order to reveal the altered shape of the institution he inhabits.

Several characteristics of Mr. Reagan are separable from the post-modern presidency. For example, there are the particular skills generally associated with Ronald Reagan as the "Great Communicator": a long career in radio, movie and television acting, time on the General Electric corporate goodwill circuit, and several years as a political commentator.[9] Few politicians, even those adept at the media arts, possess his consummate ease and skill before a camera. Second, Mr. Reagan has long stood for Reaganism—that is, a particular brand of conservative political philosophy. He has been the chief spokesman of American conservatism at least since 1965, so he has a set of well-defined and well-articulated principles to guide him and his followers in their conduct of public affairs. Few American politicians share anything similar.[10] Finally, Ronald Reagan's approach to running the White House, which has been described by admirers as like a "chairman of the board" and by critics as "detached,"[11] is not necessarily transferrable. Mr. Reagan delegates a considerable amount of power to his senior aides, and reserves for himself the role of providing overall guidance and the making of ultimate decisions. Not every president operates in this way. Even if they do not go to the extremes of Lyndon Johnson (who worked two eight-hour shifts a day) or Jimmy Carter (who insisted on checking the math on budget estimates and controlling the schedule of the White House tennis courts), other presidents will probably operate in a different fashion. While certain features of White House management leave legacies, such as Nixon's abolition of the Office of Economic Opportunity, presidential management style varies with each incumbent.[12]

After clearing away these and other Reagan-specific features of the contemporary presidency, as well as allowing for the particular circumstances and events of the day, a picture of the post-modern presidency emerges. Its shape is discernible through six characteristics that distinguish the contemporary office: 1) the revival of presidential prerogative power; 2) governing through public politics; 3) the president's general secretariat; 4) vicarious policymaking; 5) the president as chief whip in Congress; and, 6) the new vice-presidency. These features will be surveyed below, and then examined in greater detail in Chapters 4–7.

THE REVIVAL OF PREROGATIVE POWER

Presidential prerogative power took a beating in the 1970s, and not without some provocation. Presidential conduct of the Vietnam War, Richard Nixon's impoundment of funds appropriated by Congress, his invoking of executive priviledge to protect himself during Watergate, the "dirty tricks" of Nixon's reelection staff, and the apparently chronic secrecy and lying that had marked the Johnson and Nixon presidencies— all stimulated Congress to try to rein in the Chief Executive through limits on his autonomy.

As a result, a number of laws were passed and actions taken as the resurgent Congress struck at prerogative power: the War Powers Resolution, the Case Act (requiring reporting of executive agreements), the Budget and Impoundment Act of 1974 (essentially preventing impoundment), the National Commitments Resolution (calling for all significant foreign-policy commitments to be made in agreement with Congress), the legislated end to the Vietnam War, prohibition of American involvement in the Angolan civil war, and an overall resistance to unilateral presidential action.[13]

By 1979, Richard Pious could ask bluntly, "Is presidential power poison?"[14] When he did, the question seemed an unremarkable one.

Indeed, to many, it appeared to carry a natural corollary: "Is presidential power possible?" After the fall of the "imperial" presidency and the years of the "imperiled" presidency under Gerald Ford and Jimmy Carter,[15] strength in the Chief Executive was not assumed to be natural or necessarily good for the political system.

Even in the face of this apparent decline of executive power, however, a revival of presidential prerogative was underway. Ronald Reagan certainly accelerated and expanded that renaissance, but he did not begin it. For presidential prerogatives, some subtle and others blunt, have grown substantially over the last several years.

Foreign Policy Prerogatives

Presidential autonomy in foreign-policy making was a major source of contention over the "imperial" presidency, from war powers to secrecy to control over negotiations and international agreement-making.[16] Therefore, critics of that autonomy sought to restrain it through legislation.[17] While they were successful to some degree, they were nevertheless unable to eradicate prerogative powers that developed out of loopholes in the laws and court decisions favorable to the presidency.

Every law creates its own loopholes. Such is the case with the War Powers Resolution, which was designed to limit forces committed to combat without congressional approval.[18] But in practice, the law has required only that presidents be more cautious in their use of force, and either keep U.S. involvement brief (so as to avoid the law's 60-day time limit) or seek congressional approval for extended action. In the 1975 *Mayaguez* incident, the 1980 raid on Tehran, the 1982 invasion of Grenada, and fifteen other relevant incidents since the law's passage, presidential military action was unrestrained by the War Powers Resolution.[19]

In the case of President Reagan's dispatch of U. S. Marines to Beirut in 1983, a compromise was created whereby Congress approved an extended (beyond 60 days) commitment of U. S. forces, but the president never actually acknowledged the necessity of Congressional approval under the law.[20] As long as presidents avoid a confrontation with Congress on a long-term, Vietnam-type commitment (which does not seem a problem in the face of a current public antipathy to such commitments), they are relatively free to act—provided, of course, that they are subtle and choose their battles wisely.

There is, however, a difference between this situation and the pre-Resolution presidency. Post-modern presidents may need to be more circumspect in their use of force, but they now possess an effective license to commit U. S. troops without congressional approval. Earlier presidents had no such license.

In the same way, attempts to restrain presidential autonomy through the Arms Control and Disarmament Act (1961) and the Case Act (1972) have created loopholes for imaginative presidential action in the area of arms control. These acts were constructed to restrict the president's ability to commit the United States to international agreements without the acknowledgment of Congress,[21] yet for six years (1980–1986) the nation observed the limits of the unratified SALT II treaty. In short, Presidents Carter and Reagan took advantage of loopholes to achieve arms control by presidential fiat.[22]

The means for doing this was a device known as parallel unilateral policy declarations (PUPD). In January 1980, President Carter was forced by circumstances to ask the Senate to suspend consideration of his SALT II treaty. The United States and the Soviet Union then issued separate statements, identical in language, stating that each would abide by the treaty provided that the other side did likewise. By means of this "nonagreement," the terms of the treaty were in force without ratification or even formal reporting to Congress.[23]

President Carter had used this same device in 1977, when the SALT I agreement expired but SALT II was not yet complete.[24] At that time, there were protests in Congress, but some sympathetic congressional leaders stopped any legislative response. So, the 1980 action was justified by the 1977 precedent. The result was unilateral presidential policymaking for arms control, in the face of otherwise restrictive laws. In consequence, upon assuming office in 1981, President Reagan reaffirmed Carter's PUPD and continued observance of SALT II.[25] In 1985 he even extended the life of the treaty through a similar means, when the agreement's text scheduled it to expire. Then in 1986, Mr. Reagan decided to end U. S. compliance.

In the process, American arms control policy became in effect a presidential prerogative. Whereas until 1977 arms control was considered too important to be conducted without Congress (who as early as 1961 had demanded a role), by 1986 executive officials could speak of a future of arms control without agreements.[26] This, of course, implied arms control without Congress.

Loopholes alone, however, were not the only source of revived prerogative power. In 1983 the Supreme Court's ruling in the case of *INS v. Chadha* cast doubt that Congress would be able to order a president to halt military action through a concurrent resolution under the terms of the War Powers Resolution, because such "legislative vetoes" were unconstitional.[27] In 1979 the Court also struck down Senator Goldwater's challenge to President Carter's termination of the mutual defense treaty with Taiwan. The Court's ambiguous ruling seemed to establish a new presidential prerogative to end treaties.[28]

So, the presidency of the 1980s possesses an apparent license to engage in limited military action, to determine arms control policy, and to end treaties. These are new prerogatives.

Budgetary Prerogatives

Another important feature of the post-modern presidency is the new importance of budgetary policymaking. Presidential action, use of the Office of Management and Budget (OMB), and the Balanced Budget Act of 1985 (Gramm-Rudman-Hollings) have won for the president expanded prerogatives in the executive budget process.

Executive budget making, once centered in the departments and agencies and largely incremental in nature, is now dominated by the White House. Indeed, it is best characterized as "top-down" budgeting: budget decision making is centered in the president and his OMB director, who direct executive branch units in their preparation of budget requests.[29]

The impetus for this change was twofold. First, presidents have long sought to acquire centralized power over budget preparation, because budget requests reflect government priorities in the allocation of federal revenue. The more centralized is the system of executive budgeting, the more potential a president has to put his stamp on policy.[30] This fact has lead presidents to attempt to exercise increasing control over budget making, through the use of financial management devices such as the programming-planning-budgeting system (PPBS) under Presidents Kennedy and Johnson and "zero-based budgeting"(ZBB) under President Carter.[31] These earlier efforts were generally unsuccessful, but more recent attempts have been more effective because President Reagan made budget-cutting a top priority and improved computer technology helped OMB acquire the necessary data to direct budget preparation.[32]

Budget-cutting aided centralization because decentralized, incremental budgeting is most effective at maintaining the status quo. For President Reagan to advance his ambitious goal of domestic spending reductions and defense increases, he needed a government-wide perspective on budget preparation. OMB provided that perspective. Moreover, development of the Central Budget Management System (CBMS), a highly sophisticated computer system that keeps track of budget proposals and alternatives, gave OMB the technical capacity to assist the president. Through his first OMB director, David Stockman, Mr. Reagan was able to impose a "top-down" budgeting system on the traditional executive budget process. While this new approach has not been without its problems, it has given the White House the ability to dominate executive budget making.

The second impetus for change was the revision of the congressional budget process. In the 1974 Congressional Budget and Impoundment Act and the 1985 Balanced Budget Act, Congress centralized, rationalized, and disciplined its own budget procedures in order to exercise greater control over federal spending policy and compete with the presidency. The consequence of those changes was to facilitate executive budget centralization. As the newly formed congressional budget committees became the focus of legislative decision making on spending, the role of the OMB and thus the president in executive-legislative budget "politicking" was enhanced. The president, through his budget office, now plays a leading role in all aspects of the budget process, from preparing estimates and program requests to lobbying Congress to determining automatic spending cuts. The days of decentralized fiscal policymaking are gone.

Another potential prerogative in this area developed independently. The Supreme Court's ruling in *INS v. Chadha*, casting doubt on the legislative veto, could impair Congress' ability to stop presidential spending deferrals. In 1974 Budget Act gave either house of Congress the power to stop a presidential deferral of spending, but the *Chadha* ruling appears to undercut that authority. In January 1987 an appellate court struck down the president's power to defer spending unilaterally, but the Supreme Court might not accept that judgment.[33] If the high court affirms the *Chadha* decision's restrictions on the legislative veto, the result, as one Representative possibly overstated it, is that the president "winds up with what is in effect a 'line-item veto.' "[34] Spending for long-term projects, as in public works and military procurement, could be postponed indefinitely.

Administrative Clearance

The expansion of federal government activities in the twentieth century, particularly since the 1960s, has meant an explosion of administrative activities. Administrative rulemaking has become the most common form of federal legislative activity, far outstripping the lawmaking efforts of Congress. To cope with this rulemaking, the post-modern presidency now possesses the power to review and delay all rules proposed by executive agencies.

The process of administrative clearance, as this review is known, had its origins in the 1970s, but was consolidated by President Reagan in Executive Orders 12,291 (1981)[35] and 12,498 (1985).[36] Through OMB, particularly its Office of Information and Regulatory Affairs (OIRA), E. O. 12,291 requires all proposed agency rules to be reviewed and justified in terms of cost/benefit analysis.[37] In addition, E. O. 12,498 requires each agency subject to the earlier Order[38] to develop a "Regulatory Program" that specifies "all significant regulatory actions . . . planned or underway, including . . . the development of documents that may influence, anticipate, or could lead to the commencement of rulemaking proceedings."[39] The result is a potentially powerful tool for presidential control of the executive branch.

In the Reagan administration, these Orders have been used primarily to limit the rulemaking actions of the Environmental Protection Agency.[40] But another president with a different agenda could use this tool to affect other departments and agencies. For example, President Reagan exempts the Department of Defense from the administrative clearance process. Another president might not do so.

However enforced, these Executive Orders give the post-modern presidency the potential to exercise much greater control over the administrative state than did its predecessors.[41] Each year, OMB reviews about 2,500 federal regulations. Of these, 85 percent are approved without changes, 12 percent approved with changes, and the rest rejected.[42] Significantly, however, the effect of the Orders extends beyond acceptance or rejection: agency rulemakers must now consider OMB's powers and the president's views in their rulemaking process. Future presidents are unlikely to want to maintain this power.

The State of Post-Modern Prerogatives

Prerogative power is back. From military force and arms control to budgeting and regulation, the post-modern presidency possesses powers not held earlier in the twentieth century. These prerogatives do not guarantee a president success in achieving his goals, but they will give future Chief Executives additional leverage and autonomy in their efforts to shape public policy.

GOVERNING THROUGH PUBLIC POLITICS

Another feature of the post-modern presidency is its reliance on public politics for influencing the direction of policy. That reliance is a recent phenomenon, but nevertheless an important one.

The presidency, was not created necessarily to be an office of public leadership, and indeed part of the reasoning behind the Electoral College was to insulate the executive from public support.[43] Yet it soon became such an office, at least from the time of Andrew Jackson's election. If not all presidents since then have been great popular leaders, it was not because the presidency was a remote institution.

The connection between presidents and the public intensified in the twentieth century, as the rise of mass society, expanded federal government activities, and new technology all changed the nature of American politics. In response to these changes, Woodrow Wilson developed the doctrine of the "rhetorical presidency."[44] This doctrine consists of the view that the president ought to be the nation's chief policymaker, and that his policy leadership is founded on his popular election and public opinion leadership.[45]

The rhetorical presidency became the prevailing model of presidential behavior in the twentieth century, but it was significantly amended by the view expressed in Richard Neustadt's 1960 observation that "presidential power is the power to persuade."[46] On the surface, Neustadt's point seems to be but an extension of the rhetorical presidency, but it is not. For his emphasis was on presidential persuasion of others in government, specifically Congress and the bureaucracy. This persuasion is based on bargaining: the president achieves his political and policy goals by bargaining for what he wants.[47] Neustadt's argument was based on an analysis of how FDR, Truman, and Eisenhower all succeeded or failed to advance their presidential goals. He observed that presidential uses of "command" were ultimately counterproductive, and he included public appeals among the aspects of command. The result of Neustadt's observation was a new understanding of how the presidency operates: while the president was assumed to be the nation's chief policymaker and public opnion leader (or should be), his success was seen as depending on his skills at bargaining.[48]

This understanding was accepted as a summary of political reality in the modern American political system. Moreover, Lyndon Johnson, so adept at the sort of persuasion discussed by Neustadt,[49] appeared to confirm the theory: passage of Johnson's Great Society programs through Congress depended in no small part on his bargaining skills.[50]

In more recent years, however, presidential practice has moved away from the bargaining/persuasion theory. Instead, Presidents Nixon, Carter, and Reagan have all exhibited a tendency to govern through public politics. This practice of "going public," as Samuel Kernell terms it, involves presidential appeals to the American public for support for himself and his policies.[51] Rather than rely on bargaining, these presidents have appealed to the public to "tell your senators and representatives by phone, wire, and Mailgram that the future hangs in balance"[52] and that Congress should support the president's policies.

In one sense, "going public" appears to be an extension to the sort of rhetorical presidency Wilson envisioned.[53] It relies on public appeals and the president's popular electoral base. But it is more than a return to Wilson's day, for even Wilson used public appeals in a limited way. The one occasion on which he did attempt to call down public wrath on Congress, in his cross-country speaking tour on behalf of the Treaty of Versailles, demonstrates the difficulty of "going public" in the pre-television age.[54] The stress of Wilson's tour is generally thought to have ruined his health. No pre-television president could go "on the road" for every, or even most, major issues.

To that extent, "going public" is more than a continuation of the rhetorical presidency. It is probably the logical result of that doctrine, but it is also a radical intensification of it. Recent presidents have tended to "go public" more and more frequently. They have done so because of changes in the political environment and the increasing presence of political "outsiders" in the White House.[55] They have also done so because television has made it easier to reach the public: television is not only an essentially universal medium of entertainment and communications, but also the primary source of political information for most Americans.[56]

Not only is the resort to public politics a common feature of the postmodern presidency, but public support for the president is a significant determinant of presidential influence in Congress.[57] A popular president has more influence than an unpopular one. Moreover, a president who is able to mobilize public support for his policies—as Ronald Reagan did most effectively on behalf of his first budget in 1981[58]—can win important votes in Congress.

To that extent, "going public" is a significant innovation in the tactics presidents use to get their way.[59] Neustadt's idea of the "bargaining president" included a sense of the president's public support, because such support affects his standing in the capital's community of power;[60] but bargaining did not mean routine efforts by the president to go "over the heads" of other Washington figures. Bargaining proceeded primarily on the Chief Executive's willingness and ability to compromise, trade favors, promise services and favorable appointments, and employ a comprehensive understanding of the idiosyncracies of all major Washington actors.[61] Governing through public politics does not so much nullify Neustadt's point about the "power to persuade" as it provides an alternative to bargaining that is not necessarily a counterproductive command.[62] Successful use of public politics can give a president an impressive reputation, one that can aid future efforts at persuasion.[63]

Use of public politics does not, however guarantee success. Jimmy Carter resorted frequently to public appeals, but to little avail. From his early energy speeches, to his "national malaise" address, to the signing of the Camp David accords, a significant portion of the Carter presidency was conducted on the air and in prime time. Yet he could barely move Congress and was resoundingly defeated in his bid for reelection.

Nevertheless, governing through public politics is a significant aspect of the contemporary presidency. It not only means that the Chief Executive's influence is more vulnerable to swings in public opinion, but that presidential efforts to build popular support are also a major feature of the post-modern presidency. These include protection and manipulation of the presidential image, such as the careful staging of public appearances, "photo opportunities," and controlled press conferences.

Post-modern presidents not only use public politics to govern, but also realize that the entire public face of the presidency affects their ability to do so.[64]

THE PRESIDENT'S GENERAL SECRETARIAT

The post-modern presidency has at its disposal a sort of general secretariat, that is, a central staff that enables the Chief Executive to direct and supervise the work of the Executive Branch. This "secretariat" is better known as the Executive Office of the President (EOP), and in recent years it has developed into an important support staff for presidential government.[65] While the EOP has been a significant feature of the presidency ever since its creation under FDR, the contemporary Executive Office occupies a much larger role in contemporary government than it did in earlier years. It is now a powerful, bureaucratic, and politicized extension of the president.

The "general secretariat" of the post-modern presidency makes possible White House dominance of Executive Branch policymaking. It not only enables the president to play a leading role in policy formulation, but it also facilitates legislative and administrative aggressiveness by the president, provides political support for him and his policies, and generally serves to advance the president's interests.[66] This dominance can be seen through two important trends in national executive politics: the rise of OMB as a force in policymaking and implementation, and the institutionalization of the National Security Council (NSC) as a key agency in the foreign-defense policy arena.

OMB began life as the Bureau of the Budget (BoB), created by the Budget and Accounting Act of 1921 to act as a central office for collecting executive agency budget requests and transmitting them to Congress. Originally housed in the Treasury, it moved to the EOP under Franklin Roosevelt. There it has remained, acquiring additional responsibilities. In 1970 it became the OMB. At that time, President Nixon sought to give the agency a larger role in federal management improvement efforts, and the OMB Director's growing importance was reflected in a new requirement of Senate confirmation for appointment.[67]

BoB had grown in importance in the years before 1970, but in the last decade it has moved beyond its original administrative domain into the realm of policy. Indeed, in the first Reagan Administration it was considered the most important component of the EOP.[68] While that preeminence probably will not remain through future presidencies, OMB's policy role is now well established.[69]

The reasons for that importance all revolve around the growing importance of budgetary issues in the U. S. government. As the budget has grown more and more to be the focus of policy decision making, so OMB's influence has increased. Thus a large role for the budget office was somewhat inevitable, no matter who became president in 1980. But the election of Ronald Reagan and his subsequent battles with Congress over the budget guaranteed OMB a major role into the future.[70] The legacy of those battles was the establishment of a long-term deficit problem for the nation, thus ensuring OMB's significance in future policymaking.[71] The Balanced Budget Act of 1985, or anything that may replace it (even "no-deficit" targets), increases that significance.[72]

OMB's influence also extends beyond budgets. It has long operated a legislative clearance process, whereby the office's Legislative Reference Division coordinates, reviews, and clears hundreds of legislative proposals that emanate annually from executive agencies to Congress. The Division also reviews agency reports to Congress, testimony on proposed laws, and informs congressional committees of how pending legislation relates to the president's program. Finally, it advises the president on bills readied for his signature or veto.[73] In short, legislative clearance is a major tool for presidential control of the Executive Branch.

Administrative clearance arose in the 1970s to complement legislative review. Because of the growing volume and significance of federal executive regulations, presidents since Richard Nixon have attempted to control rulemaking by administrative agencies. Nixon required Quality of Life Review, intended for the most part to reconcile the rules issued by the Environmental Protection Agency with other administration goals.[74] President Ford required that all agencies assess and report on the inflationary impact of "major" proposed rules, with OMB responsible for overseeing compliance.[75] Jimmy Carter expanded the scope of review even more, and established a Regulatory Council to coordinate the rulemaking and review process.[76] No one agency, however, had supervisory power over agencies except the agencies themselves. All that changed with the Reagan administrative clearance process, described above, which has consolidated OMB dominion over the review process. Because the rise of administrative clearance has been a long-term trend, and because it gives the president the capacity for Executive Branch control, this centralized review will likely continue to characterize the post-modern presidency.[77]

The recent rise of OMB is complemented by the institutionalization of the National Security Council. The NSC, both through its staff and as a forum for policy coordination, now serves as an important component of the foreign and defense policy decision process. It enables the president to oversee all aspects of that process, maintain a "presidential" perspective on security issues,[78] and balance the competing interests and contributions of the State and Defense departments.[79]

NSC's institutionalization, ironically, came after its chief staff member had already secured a prominent place in the president's foreign-policy government. The Assistant to the President for National Security Affairs[80] rose to some importance under Kennedy and Johnson, although both presidents avoided using the NSC as a formal structure.[81] President Nixon's "NSC system" centralized all foreign-policy decision processes in his Assistant, Henry Kissinger.[82] Kissinger's tenure represents the climax of power for the Assistant: he was more influential than the secretaries of State and Defense. After that "Lone Ranger" approach drew heavy criticism for usurping the authority of traditional foreign and defense policy institutions, President Ford reduced the influence of the Assistant. Under Presidents Carter and Reagan, the Assistant's role has been that of a strong actor among other strong actors, especially the State and Defense secretaries.[83] Under President Reagan, the NSC staff was even used for managing covert operations in the Iran-Contra arms affair. These activities have ceased, but reflect the significance of the NSC staff to presidential policymaking.

In the last three administrations, the NSC has also provided an agency for coordinating decision making in all areas of national security affairs. It has thus been institutionalized; in other words, its role has been secured and made permanent. Most of the value of the NSC appears to lie in the ability of the Assistant and his staff to expose the president to the range of opinions and options relevant to his decisions. Future presidents will not ignore the NSC because they need that support.

These two trends in executive politics, the rise of the OMB and the institutionalization of the NSC, are related to two seemingly contradictory developments in the structure and operations of the EOP. To be specific, in recent years the Executive Office has become institutionalized and at the same time politicized. On the one hand, the EOP has been institutionalized:[84] it has grown larger and more complex in recent

years, and "crystallized" through the creation of a number of more-
or-less permanent components. The contemporary EOP consists of ten
units, four of which have been created since 1969.[85] In addition, as
noted above, OMB was reorganized in 1970 and has acquired new
organization, status, and power unknown at an earlier date.[86] Finally,
the White House Office has grown larger and more complex in recent
years, acquiring among other components an Office of Public Liaison
and an Office of Communications.[87]

The other development, politicization, is apparently contradictory
because many observers regard politicization as deinstitutionalization.[88]
This analysis focuses on the fact that several components of the EOP—
OMB in particular—had previously developed as nonpartisan, professional agencies of the presidency. In recent years, these agencies have
been transformed into support staffs for the political and policy interests
of the president of the day. OMB is now an integral part of that "general
secretariat," promoting the president's agenda.[89]

The apparent contradiction disappears, however, when one realizes
that the de-institutionalization of presidential agencies is the institutionalization of the presidency itself. What was called the institutionalization of the presidency for many years (i.e., the expansion of
nonpartisan professional staffs in EOP) was really the institutionalization
of EOP agencies. Critics may bemoan the decline of nonpartisan staff
units, but presidents want to protect and promote their own interests.
Thus, the "politicized presidency" that has developed in recent years
is an extension of the incumbent.[90] Its existence allows him to act in
his own interest.

The institutionalization of the presidency, then, is what the development of this "general secretariat" is all about. The EOP is big,
bureaucratic, and powerful, but it has become so in order to support
the president. For better or worse—and the choice between them is not
clear—the presidency now possesses a greater capacity for controlling
Executive Branch policymaking.[91]

As a result, presidents need more help to operate and manage this
"general secretariat." Such control requires more formal organization
and hierarchy of staff than some presidents have desired. Where Kennedy and Johnson could eschew formal structures and disparage "bureaucracy" in the White House, Jimmy Carter—after emulating them
for a while—was forced to appoint a Chief of Staff.[92] President Reagan
never attempted to run the White House without such an aide, in part

because of his management style but also because of his acceptance of this fact.

So, the post-modern presidency has a general secretariat to advance presidential interests. That secretariat, as it were, enhances presidential and managerial skills on the part of the president. As a result, post-modern presidents need a senior aide, a chief of staff, to help them make the general secretariat work.

VICARIOUS POLICYMAKING

The post-modern presidency not only makes policy through direct actions of the Chief Executive, the White House staff, and OMB, but also through the president's appointments to positions in the federal judiciary and independent regulatory commissions. Such influence is a kind of vicarious policymaking.

Vicarious policymaking occurs when a president's influence is felt through the actions and decisions of his appointees, particularly those who have independent power to make authoritative governmental decisions. In such cases, the president either takes vicarious pleasure in seeing his appointees make policy as he would wish it to be made, or experiences disappointment because someone he named to office has acted in a way contrary to his expectations. Recent presidents have seen both: President Nixon got what he expected when he named William Rehnquist to the Supreme Court, while Dwight Eisenhower regarded as one of his greatest mistakes the appointment of Earl Warren as Chief Justice.

Long after a president is gone, his influence may be felt through the work of his appointees, whether or not he would agree with them, because he put them in office.[93] This fact has become even more significant in recent years, as the policymaking power of courts and regulatory agencies has expanded.[94] The United States now has much more of an administrative/juridicial state than it did even twenty years ago.

Like all vicarious experiences, however, this sort of policymaking is often unsatisfying. It is so because someone else is doing it, and especially if the someone else is doing something the appointing president does not want done. Moreover, policymaking by appointment is a terribly blunt instrument: first, a president can never be sure exactly how his appointees will act or decide in the future; and, second, individual presidential appointees cannot always make a dramatic difference in the policies controlled by the respective court or agency.

The main point here, however, is more a qualitative than a quantitative one. It is that a considerable portion of a president's impact on the governance of the United States is in what his appointees do. Whether a president makes a few regulatory/judicial appointments or many, those choices will help to shape important policy decisions for years to come. A single vote on a commission or the Supreme Court can shape a policy ruling that will have far-reaching effects: dictating rules governing abortions, requiring a product be withdrawn from the market, mandating a higher interest rate, and a host of other significant and binding policy decisions.

Of course, appointments have always been important to presidents and their desire to shape the course of national policy. A good example of this fact is from the tenure of John Adams. While otherwise limited in his ability to make a lasting impression on government, probably Adams' most important action as president was to appoint John Marshall as Chief Justice of the United States.[95] In the same way, President Eisenhower's appointment of Earl Warren to the position of Chief Justice probably had a more significant long-term effect on domestic policy than legislative initiatives during Ike's eight years in the White House.

So, what is different about today that makes vicarious policymaking a feature of the post-modern presidency? If appointments have always been potentially significant, are contemporary conditions really anything new?

The answer to that last question is a guarded "yes." Appointments may have always been potentially important, but in recent years the power of the judiciary and regulatory agencies has expanded.

Judicial power underwent great expansion in the 1950s and 1960s, in the days of the Warren Court, but it was not until the Burger Court of the 1970s was it clear that judicial activism would be a more-or-less permanent feature of U. S. government. John Agresto succinctly stated the reasons for this conclusion in 1984:

Since Warren Burger has become chief justice, the Court has voided federal legislation in over three dozen instances, nullified more acts of Congress on First Amendment grounds than all of its predecessors combined, unanimously overruled the president on warrantless electronic surveillance, curtailed his activity on such issues as executive privilege and impoundment, declared for the first time that busing may be used to overcome segregation in schools, greatly expanded the protection against gender-related discrimination, upset the various state procedures on the death penalty, and voided scores of antiabortion statutes.[96]

The Supreme Court of the late twentieth century is thus more powerful than ever before, and a national policymaking body. In consequence, lower federal courts and a number of state courts (most notably, the California Supreme Court) have also become activist policymakers.

The power of administrative and regulatory agencies expanded in the 1970s, as Congress delegated broad rulemaking power to a number of executive and independent units.[97] The Federal Trade Commission's (FTC) powers, for example, were expanded in 1974 under the Moss-Magnuson Act:[98] the Commission was empowered to issue Trade Regulation Rules that govern industry trade practices, a power it has used extensively.[99]

At the same time that the power of the administrative state was growing, however, Congress sought it tame it through use of the legislative veto.[100] For a time, the veto seemed a perfect solution: it gave Congress, or some part of it, the power to halt unwise or impolitic applications of broad regulatory authority. But the 1983 Supreme Court decision in *INS v. Chadha* fouled that solution, and the legislative veto as it was practiced is no longer available. There are substitutes for it, from requiring congressional approval for any proposed regulations to delaying the implementation of rules, but none of them will be as convenient or as seemingly effective for overseeing the regulators as the legislative veto.[101] All potential substitutes will require more time and effort by Congress, commodities that are in terribly short supply in the modern legislature.

So, the subjects of presidential appointments, the courts and regulatory commissions, are more powerful now than they were once. Thus, appointments are potentially more significant than they once were.

No matter how presidents handle this vicarious life, the choices they make will cast long shadows. President Reagan believed this to be true, and put great effort into placing his kind of incumbents in office (Rehnquist and Scalia on the Supreme Court, James Miller at the FTC, and others). Other post-modern presidents may or may not be as aggressive in their attempts to shape policy vicariously, but whatever they do will stand as a concrete contribution to the shaping of national policy. Call it the "surrogate presidency."

THE PRESIDENT AS CHIEF WHIP IN CONGRESS

If he is to succeed in his relations with Congress, a post-modern president must go farther than his predecessors to develop his influence in that body. He must act in effect as the chief whip in Congress.

Presidential relations with Congress have never been simple. From the time of Washington's difficulties with the early Senate to modern battles between the first and second branches over the budget,[102] the president and Congress have had a complex and often stormy relationship.

Modern presidents, however, have been expected to take a leading role in influencing the course of legislation. Indeed, presidential leadership of Congress (to use a popular term) is one of the general characteristics of the post-FDR presidency. To that end, modern presidents developed or attempted to cultivate good relations with congressional leaders and powerful members.[103]

Where their predecessors could work with powerful committee "barons" and influential members to write laws, post-modern presidents find a very different situation. The open Congress of the late twentieth century is a place of much greater decentralization than the legislature of even two decades before. As a result of changes in rules and customs during the 1970s,[104] the contemporary Congress is a place of fragmented power. A post-modern president cannot rely on powerful members such as a Wilbur Mills or Richard Russell to deliver votes, nor count on predictable alignments of members (such as Southern Democrats) in calculating legislative strategy.[105]

The president must now act as "chief whip" to build his own coalitions. Decentralization means that presidential bargaining with Congress is more difficult, because the Chief Executive must deal with so many members and their staffs. On the other hand, the absence of the old centers of power means that it is more difficult for Congress to ignore a popular president's requests.

What must a president do to cope with this new Congress? Several points are clear. First, as Norman Ornstein has noted:

To prevail these days, a president first must accept a cardinal premise: he will be required to know and to deal regularly with a much wider array of players in the process, members *and* staff. Such dealings require a congressional liaison staff that works to know not just who the members are, but what they like and dislike, who needs to be sweet-talked and who can be bullied, who will be satisfied with a special White House tour for constituents or an invitation to a state dinner and who will insist on a substantive concession. Knowing the members also means maintaining an active, ongoing intelligence operation to achieve early warning of who might introduce a surprise amendment or oppose a presidential initiative or be vulnerable at a given future moment to a particular presidential plea.[106]

All of this resembles the kind of information and skills associated with a legislative whip. If a president is not willing to act as one, he runs a serious risk of failing with Congress. Jimmy Carter's early problems with Congress can be directly attributed to his misunderstanding of Ornstein's cardinal premise.[107]

But the president cannot be chief whip alone. He needs an effective legislative liaison staff to give him information and do a lot of the head-counting and cajoling involved in building a coalition. The president and his liaison staff must understand Congress and its operations if they are to make it work for them.[108] As with a whip or any other politician who seeks influence in Congress, knowledge is the key to power, and a good staff provides the means for acquiring knowledge.

Beyond building an effective staff, however, the president must also be willing and able to do two things: 1) establish and communicate his legislative priorities; and, 2) involve himself in the process of lobbying Congress, both through bargaining and public politics. A president without clear priorities will, like Jimmy Carter, find the legislative process jammed: President Carter sent Congress a long list of proposals in 1977, but no sense of which were most important. As a result, action on all of them was stalled.[109] In contrast, Ronald Reagan's priorities were clear to legislators, so he was able to see Congress act upon them. Having priorities does not guarantee success, but not having them effectively assures failure.

The president cannot, however, announce his priorities and then retire. As chief whip, he must actively involve himself in politicking with Congress.[110] He must use the knowledge he has, the threats and favors at his disposal, and his own reputation and public standing to induce Congress to cooperate. More of the president's limited time than before must now be spent in "working" Congress: making phone calls, meeting with members, maintaining close relations with congressional leaders, and other related activities. Being the whip is a demanding job.

Of course, traditional political skills of timing and bargaining are relevant, but post-modern presidents must work harder to make Congress work for them. They can make use of the revived prerogative powers of the office and public politics to great effect, but they cannot ignore Congress in the process. Because the contemporary Congress is so different from the old legislature of Richard Russell and Sam Rayburn, contemporary presidents must alter their approach to legislative relations accordingly.

THE NEW VICE-PRESIDENCY

The final characteristic of the post-modern presidency is the new vice-presidency. The past two decades have seen the transformation of the republic's Second Citizen from a minor political figure into an important presidential advisor.[111]

In the wake of Watergate and Gerald Ford's accession to the presidency, followed by two "outsider" presidents in Washington, the vice-presidency has become a position that offers its incumbent an opportunity to be among that small circle of senior presidential aides and counselors.[112] The last three vice-presidents, particularly Walter Mondale and George Bush, have demonstrated a potential for influence in the office that was long ridiculed for its unimportance. They have done so because the presidents they served were willing to allow them a larger role than their predecessors. Moreover, since both Presidents Carter and Reagan were "outsiders" in Washington, their "insider" seconds provided useful information and connections to the centers of power in the capital.

As a result, the vice-president has become a useful advisor to the president, someone who can offer the Chief Executive the benefit of his knowledge of public issues, the policy process, and political strategy.[113] Moreover, the vice-president's institutional resources for such an activist role have been enhanced. Rockefeller, Mondale, and Bush were all guaranteed unlimited access to their president, and by using that privilege (not always granted in the past) wisely each was able to stay closely in touch with the daily business of the White House. The vice-president's staff has also increased: once small and ill-equipped to contribute to policymaking, it is now a staff of about seventy or eighty professionals.[114] So, the Second Citizen of the nation can now contribute to national government as never before.

How is this trend significant? It is important for several reasons. First, the vice-presidency is now a better preparation for the top job than ever before, should an emergency accession occur. Where Harry Truman came to the Oval Office unaware of the Manhattan Project and Lyndon Johnson had little knowledge of the workings of the Kennedy White House, post-modern vice-presidents are better prepared for becoming the Chief. With an attempted presidential assassination as recently as 1981, the need is great for a successor who is at least partially prepared.[115] Moreover, with Ronald Reagan's demonstration that age is no obstacle to a successful run for the presidency, there may well be more older candidates and presidents. In consequence, the need for someone who can assume the mantle of office is not an incidental one.[116]

Second, since the new electoral politics that has developed in the last two decades has restored to "outsiders" a serious chance of capturing the White House, "insider" seconds will probably be valuable into the future. It was not too long ago that pundits scoffed at the notion of governors or even ex-governors winning the presidency. The last two presidents, however, have been in the latter category, and non-Washington politicians are now routinely among those "mentioned" as potential nominees for both parties.[117] As presidents, these figures will want advice from their vice-presidents, who are likely to be Washington "insiders" of some stature.

Third, the other developments that characterize the post-modern presidency all contribute to a Chief Executive's need for an activist second. As this chapter has made clear, a president in the late twentieth century is called upon to deal with a new and more difficult Congress, use public politics skillfully, preside over a large and powerful "general secretariat," employ a wide array of prerogative powers, and influence national policy vicariously, all at the same time. He needs a chief of staff to help him keep up with all of these responsibilities, and can use the sort of advice that the senior politician called the vice-president has to offer. So, it is likely that the new vice-presidency is here to stay. It fits well with the altered shape of the presidency.

Of course, the price of admission for prospective vice-presidents has not changed. They must first contribute to the electability of the nominees who choose them. Whether to balance sectional, ideological, ethnic, or whatever interests, vice-presidential candidates are chosen to assist party nominees in winning the presidential election. Once in office, a second price must be paid: the vice-president must demonstrate exemplary loyalty to his Chief. Walter Mondale and George Bush were activist vice-presidents precisely because their bosses never had to question their loyalty. Any politician who will not pay that price will be relegated to the status of Lyndon Johnson in the Kennedy Administration. Mistrusted and not respected by Kennedy's men, LBJ suffered the worst years of his political career.[118]

For those who can pay the price of admission, however, the vice-presidency now offers greater rewards than it once did. It offers the chance of making of a real contribution to the workings of the post-modern presidency.

This, then, is the shape of the contemporary presidency. As the preceding survey has demonstrated, much has changed about the office in the past two decades. The changes have not been so drastic as to suggest that an entirely new phase of the presidency has begun, but there have been alterations in the office. The best term for capturing and labelling these changes is to refer to the institution today as the post-modern presidency.

In Chapters 4–7, the various aspects of the post-modern presidency will be examined in depth. But before these features can be understood, the post-modern presidency must be placed in context. Placing it requires an understanding of what happened to change the modern presidency, as well as a sense of how the contemporary political environment is different from the politics of "midcentury" (as Richard Neustadt called the 1950s and 1960s). Chapters 2 and 3 will tell those stories.

This post-modern presidency owes something to Ronald Reagan, but he is certainly not its sole creator. Rather, he has consolidated a number of trends and added his own twists to the shaping of the presidency. Presidents after Mr. Reagan will find the office different than it used to be.

NOTES

1. Charles O. Jones, "Keeping faith and losing Congress: The Carter experience in Washington," *Presidential Studies Quarterly* 14 (Summer 1984): 441–444, argues that a new policy agenda had been in the works for several years. I agree, but think that Ronald Reagan's effect on the political agenda

was important: he consolidated the trends into a new political reality. This is best seen in the large number of works written to document and analyze Mr. Reagan's influence on the direction of American public policy. Many of these works tell the tale in their titles. See John E. Chubb and Paul E. Peterson, eds., *The New Direction in American Politics* (Washington: The Brookings Institution, 1985); John L. Palmer and Elizabeth V. Sawhill, eds., *The Reagan Experiment* (Washington: Urban Institute Press, 1982); and Lawrence I. Barrett, *Gambling With History: Reagan in the White House* (New York: Penguin Books, 1984). Other works, with less titillating titles, have looked at Mr. Reagan's effect on American politics. See, for example, Fred Greenstein, ed., *The Reagan Presidency: An Early Assessment* (Baltimore: Johns Hopkins University Press, 1982); Norman J. Ornstein, ed., *President and Congress: Assessing Reagan's First Year* (Washington: American Enterprise Institute, 1982); Lester M. Salamon and Michael S. Lund, *The Reagan Presidency and the Governing of America* (Washington: Urban Institute Press, 1984); and, John L. Palmer and Elizabeth V. Sawhill, eds., *The Reagan Record* (Washington: Ballinger, 1984). The above list is meant to be illustrative rather than exhaustive: since 1980, there has been a cottage industry of books on Reagan, the Reagan Administration, and Reaganism. The author apologizes for adding one more to the heap, but hopes the difference of focus will justify this book.

2. Mondale's rhetoric in 1984 still echoed all the themes of traditional Democratic New Dealism, but in reality his claim to the presidency was made largely on the issue of "fairness." For the first time in recent memory, the Democratic platform of 1984 made no calls for big, new domestic spending programs. The debate of the 1984 campaign was largely on Reagan's terms. See Peter Goldman and Tony Fuller, et al., *The Quest for the Presidency 1984* (New York: Bantam Books, 1985).

3. New York *Times*, September 24, 1986, p. 12.

4. Throughout this book I shall refer to the presidency in the "late twentieth century." In his classic *Presidential Power*, (New York: John Wiley, 1980), Richard Neustadt uses the term "midcentury" to capture his sense of the time about which he was writing. I refer to my time in that spirit.

5. Erwin Hargrove and Michael Nelson, *Presidents, Politics and Policy* (Baltimore: Johns Hopkins University Press, 1984), Chapter 1. See also even as recent a work as Harold M. Barger, *The Impossible Presidency: Illusions and Realities of Executive Power* (Glenview, IL. Scott-Foresman, 1984).

6. Lloyd Cutler, "To form a government—On the defects of separation of powers," *Foreign Affairs* 59 (Fall 1980): 126–143, as well as John Charles Daly, et al., *President vs. Congress: Does the Separation of Powers Still Work?* AEI Forum 47 (Washington: American Enterprise Institute, 1981). Of course, the "weak presidency, need for change" school of thought did not originate in the 1970s, but gained wider attention then.

7. Quoted in Joseph Kraft, "The Post-Imperial Presidency," New York *Times Magazine*, November 2, 1980, p. 31.

8. Richard Nathan, *The Administrative Presidency* (New York: John Wiley, 1983), chapters 5 and 6.

9. Mr. Reagan's pre-presidential career is described in his autobiography (written with Richard G. Hubler), *Where's the Rest of Me?* (New York: Duell, Sloan, and Pearce, 1965), and in Lou Cannon, *Reagan* (New York: Putnam, 1982).

10. My point here is *not* that Mr. Reagan has proven that ideology is an important component of presidential power, but that firm ideology is a rare trait among American political leaders. Therefore, the fact of ideology, rather than the direction of it, is a quality that must be excised when assessing Mr. Reagan's legacy for the office.

11. For a discussion of President Reagan's management style, see Nolan J. Argyle and Ryan J. Barilleaux, "Past failures and future prescriptions for Presidential management reform," *Presidential Studies Quarterly* 16 (Fall 1986): 716–733. For a critical view, see James David Barber, *The Presidential Character*, 3rd ed. (Englewood Cliffs, NJ: Prentice-Hall, 1985), pp. 464–466. At this point, I am discussing Mr. Reagan's personal approach to managing the White House, rather than White House or Executive Office organization and operations in the Reagan Administration.

12. There are, of course, tendencies and trends in White House management, but that does not mean that each president will operate his Executive Office and White House staff in exactly the same way. See Stephen Hess, *Organizing the Presidency* (Washington: The Brookings Institution, 1976); and Argyle and Barilleaux, op. cit.

13. The foreign policy aspects of this period are covered most effectively in Thomas M. Franck and Edward Weisband, *Foreign Policy by Congress* (New York: Oxford University Press, 1979). A good compendium of the foreign-policy legislation of this period is U. S. Congress, *Legislation on Foreign Relations Through 1983*, Vol. I (Washington: Government Printing Office, 1984). The domestic side of this period has been covered less comprehensively. A number of works beat around the appropriate bush, however, including the fine essays in Anthony King, ed., *Both Ends of the Avenue* (Washington: American Enterprise Institute, 1983), and idem., *The New American Political System* (Washington: American Enterprise Institute, 1978).

14. Richard Pious, *The American Presidency* (New York: Basic Books, 1979), p. 3.

15. Throughout this work, I put such terms as "imperilled" presidency and "imperial" or "post-imperial" presidency in quotes, because they are labels representing ideas with which I am not completely comfortable. Yes, presidential power expanded under Presidents Johnson and Nixon, and contracted

under Presidents Ford and Carter, but such terms are not exactly precise. Of course, neither is my term "post-modern," but I make no claims that it is anything but a conventional label.

16. See, for example, Arthur Schlesinger, Jr., *The Imperial Presidency* (New York: Popular Library, 1973). Schlesinger invented the phrase "imperial presidency" and his book is representative of a whole body of literature attacking the power of the presidency in the late 1960s and early 1970s. For an in-depth discussion of executive-legislative conflicts over the making of international agreements, see Loch K. Johnson, *The Making of International Agreements: Congress Confronts the Executive* (New York: New York University Press, 1984).

17. The relevant details of this legislation are treated effectively elsewhere. My purpose here is to discuss how it failed to restrain presidents in the fashion its architects expected. See Franck and Weisband, op. cit., for a treatment of the anti-autonomy laws.

18. The War Powers Resolution (50 U. S. C. 1542, 1543, 1982) requires the president: 1) to consult with Congress on the use of U. S. troops in hostile or even potentially hostile situations; 2) to report to Congress in writing within forty-eight hours after ordering troops into a hostile situation; 3) to cease military action sixty days after reporting to Congress, unless Congress declares war, extends the sixty-day period, or is unable to meet because of an attack on the United States; and, 4) to end the use of U. S. forces at any time if so required by a concurrent resolution of Congress. This last point was called into question by the Supreme Court's ruling in the case of *INS v. Chadha* (103 S. Ct. 2764; June 23, 1983), because the Court implied that a concurrent resolution may not be a constitutional means of restricting presidential action.

19. For a good discussion of the effectiveness of the Resolution, see Daniel Paul Franklin, "War powers in the modern context," *Congress and the Presidency* 14 (Spring 1987): 77–92.

20. Louis Fisher, *Constitutional Conflicts Between Congress and the President* (Princeton: Princeton University Press, 1985), p. 317.

21. The Arms Control and Disarmament Act of 1961 (22 U. S. C. 2573, 1982) contains a Section 33 that specifies that the United States may not enter into arms control or disarmament agreements except by treaty or "unless further authorized by further affirmative legislation by the Congress of the United States." The Case Act (1 U. S. C. 112b, 1982) requires that all international agreements other than treaties be transmitted to Congress within sixty days of their conclusion.

22. Ryan J. Barilleaux, "Executive non-agreements, arms control, and the invitation to struggle in foreign affairs," *World Affairs* 148 (Fall 1986): 217–27; idem., "Parallel unilateral policy declarations: A new device for Presidential autonomy in foreign affairs," *Presidential Studies Quarterly*: forthcoming; and, Fisher, *Constitutional Conflicts*, pp. 278–279.

23. Something like PUPD had been used by presidents at least since 1962 (see Johnson, *The Making of International Agreements*, p. 63), but such a device had never been used in so significant or so public a manner.

24. Fisher, pp. 278–279.

25. It was of course ironic that Mr. Reagan, a vocal critic of SALT II, should be the protector of the treaty for five years. But then, interest in prerogative powers is not limited by party or ideology.

26. Kenneth Adelman, "Arms control with and without agreements," *Foreign Affairs* (Winter 1984/85): 240–263. Mr. Adelman, director of the Arms Control and Disarmament Agency, was very careful to frame his comments in terms of restraint, but his suggestion is clearly tied to this (not uncontroversial, or necessarily legal) idea of PUPD:

Another approach, and to me the most promising of innovative thoughts, is arms control through individual but (where possible) parallel policies: i.e., arms control without agreements (treaties, in particular). . . . (p. 259)

See Barilleaux, "Executive non-agreements," for a review of the legal/constitutional problems involved in the use of PUPDs.

27. 103 S.Ct. 2782. See also Fisher, *Constitutional Conflicts*, p. 313; and, U. S. Congress, House, Committee on Rules, *Legislative Veto After Chadha*, hearings before the Committee on Rules, 98th Cong., 2nd sess., November 9, 1983-May 10, 1984.

28. *Goldwater v. Carter*, 444 U. S. 996 (1979). See also Fisher, pp. 270–272. As Fisher makes clear, historical practice tended to favor a congressional role in treaty termination.

29. Virginia McMurty, "OMB's role in the federal budget process," in *Office of Management and Budget: Evolving Roles and Future Issues*, prepared by the Congressional Research Service, Library of Congress (Washington: Government Printing Office, 1986), pp. 16–17; Hugh Heclo, "Executive budget making," in *Federal Budget Policy in the 1980s*, edited by Gregory B. Mills and John Palmer (Washington: Urban Institute Press, 1984), pp. 262–270; and Allen Schick, "The budget as an instrument of Presidential policy," in *The Reagan Presidency and the Governing of America*, edited by Lester M. Salamon and Michael S. Lund (Washington: Urban Institute Press, 1984).

30. These points will be explored at greater length in Chapter 3, under the section on "the budget as the central instrument for governing."

31. See Aaron Wildavsky, *The Politics of the Budgetary Process*, 4th ed. (Boston: Little, Brown, 1984), especially Chapter 6: "PPD and ZBB."

32. McMurty, loc. cit.

33. New York *Times*, January 23, 1987, p. 1.

34. *National Journal*, May 24, 1986, p. 1259.

35. 3 C. F. R. 1981 Comp., p. 127, 46 *Fed. Reg.* 13,193 (1981). The development of administrative clearance has been extremely controversial. This

work will not enter into the debate about whether or not presidents *ought* to exercise such power, but will consider whether or not they *can* do so and the consequences of their doing so.

36. 50 *Fed. Reg.* 1036 (1985).

37. The literature on administrative clearance is extensive and growing. The best sources for understanding it are Morton Rosenberg, "Regulatory management at OMB," in *Office of Management and Budget: Evolving Roles and Future Issues*; William F. West and Joseph Cooper, "The rise of administrative clearance," in *The Presidency and Public Policy Making*, edited by George Edwards III, Steven Shull, and Norman Thomas (Pittsburgh: University of Pittsburgh Press, 1985); and Howard Ball, *Controlling Regulatory Sprawl* (Westport, CT: Greenwood Press, 1984).

38. E. O. 12,291 and 12,498 apply to the Department of Agriculture, Department of Commerce, Department of Education, Department of Energy, Department of Health and Human Services, Department of Housing and Urban Development, Department of Interior, Department of Justice, Department of Labor, Department of Transportation, Department of the Treasury, Environmental Protection Agency, Equal Employment Opportunity Commission, General Services Administration, Office of Personnel Management, Small Business Administration, and the Veterans Administration. The Department of Defense and all independent regulatory agencies are not covered.

39. E. O. 12,498, sec. 2(a).

40. U. S. Congress, Senate, Committee on Environment and Public Works, *Office of Management and Budget Influence on Agency Regulations*, Committee Print, 99th Congress, 2nd session, 1986.

41. I. e., government by bureaucracy.

42. New York *Times*, December 10, 1984, p. 17.

43. Charles Thatch, *The Creation of the Presidency, 1775–1789* (Baltimore: Johns Hopkins University Press, 1969; orig. pub. 1923) pp. 167–168. See also Ruth Weissbourd Grant and Stephen Grant, "The Madisonian Presidency," and Harvey Flaumenhauft, "Hamilton's administrative republic and the American Presidency," in *The Presidency in the Constitutional Order*, edited by Joseph M. Bessette and Jeffrey Tulis (Baton Rouge: Louisiana State University Press, 1981).

44. My analysis and discussion of the "rhetorical presidency" draws heavily on the work of James Ceasar and his colleagues. See James Ceasar, Glen Thurow, Jeffrey Tulis, and Joseph Bessette, "The rise of the rhetorical Presidency," *Presidential Studies Quarterly* 11 (Spring 1981): 233–251, and James Ceasar, "The rhetorical Presidency revisited," in *Modern Presidents and the Presidency*, pp. 15–34, edited by Marc Landy (Lexington, MA: Lexington Books, 1985).

45. Popular election not necessarily in the sense of direct election by the

public, but in the sense that the Electoral College is a nondeliberative body that rubberstamps the popular winner.

46. Richard Neustadt, *Presidential Power*, revised (New York: John Wiley, 1980). The original version of this book, retained without change in subsequent editions, was first published in 1960.

47. Neustadt, op. cit. Samuel Kernell, *Going Public: New Strategies of Presidential Leadership* (Washington: Congressional Quarterly Press, 1986), p. 3, makes this point as well in his discussion of Neustadt.

48. Kernell, loc. cit.

49. Adept, at least, when it came to domestic policy, and even in foreign policy for a time.

50. These skills are usually attributed to Johnson's experience as Senate Majority Leader. See Rowland Evans and Robert Novak, *Lyndon B. Johnson: The Exercise of Power* (New York: New American Library, 1966); Doris Kearns, *Lyndon Johnson and the American Dream* (New York: Harper and Row, 1976); and, Erwin Hargrove and Michael Nelson, *Presidents, Politics, and Policy* (Baltimore: Johns Hopkins University Press, 1984).

51. Kernell, pp. 1–7. My analysis of governing through public politics draws heavily on Kernell's examination of "going public," as I have interpreted it in the context of other aspects of what George Edwards calls the "public presidency."

52. From Ronald Reagan's address to the nation on his 1986 budget, as quoted in Kernell, p. 3.

53. Ceasar and his colleagues do not interpret the rhetorical presidency as a phenomenon interrupted by Neustadt's "bargaining president," but I think that a strong case can be made to the contrary. John Kennedy read Neustadt's book and used him as an unofficial advisor. LBJ's mode of governing also relied on bargaining and persuasion. But Ceasar et al. see the rhetorical presidency as a feature of most twentieth-century administrations. I do not disagree, but I share Kernell's view that rhetoric and bargaining are different.

54. Described in Alexander L. George and Juliette L. George, *Woodrow Wilson and Colonel House* (New York: J. Day Co., 1956), pp. 290–292.

55. Discussed in Chapter 3. See also Kernell, Chapter 2: "How Washington and Presidents have changed."

56. Fred Smoller, "The six o'clock Presidency: Patterns of network news coverage of the President," *Presidential Studies Quarterly* 16 (Winter 1986): 31–49.

57. George C. Edwards III, *Presidential Influence in Congress* (San Francisco: W. H. Freeman, 1980), pp. 86–100. See also idem., *The Public President* (New York: St. Martin's, 1983), pp. 199–208.

58. Mr. Reagan's televised appeal for public support brought a flood of correspondence to the Capitol Post Office and virtually jammed the phone lines to congressional offices. Described in Kernell, pp. 115–123. See also Allen

Schick, "How the budget was won and lost," in *President and Congress: Assessing Reagan's First Year*, edited by Norman J. Ornstein (Washington: American Enterprise Institute, 1982), pp. 14–43.

59. Kernell, p. 2.

60. Neustadt, pp. 64–65.

61. Ibid., pp. 28–29. See also Kernell, pp. 15–17.

62. Of course, not everyone sees command as inevitaably counterproductive. See Peter Sperlich, "Bargaining and overload: An essay on *Presidential Power*," in *The Presidency*, pp. 168–192, edited by Aaron Wildavsky (Boston: Little, Brown, 1969). Sperlich contends that at some point a president must give orders, if only to his staff. Fred Greenstein thus incorporates Sperlich's observation into what he calls a modified version of Neustadt's theory. Fred Greenstein, "Continuity and change in the modern Presidency," in *The New American Political System*, p. 69. Gordon Hoxie makes the case for command even more bluntly: focusing on foreign and defense policy, Hoxie sees no alternative but command in a variety of policy decisions; R. Gordon Hoxie, *Command Decision and the Presidency* (New York: Reader's Digest Press, 1977), pp. xii-xiii. The overriding point, however, is that going public is not necessarily a form of command: it is not direct bargaining, but members of Congress do see a benefit in responding to public demands for presidential support (i.e., reelection, etc.). Going public may then be a "third force," to the extent that it can move Congress and even enhance a president's professional reputation.

63. Neustadt himself has come to include public appeals in his view of persuasion. The most recent revision of *Presidential Power* (in 1980) includes a discussion of Jimmy Carter's inability to make "going public" work for him. But his original study contained only one reference to anything similar, and that one in a negative light: that Truman's 1951 public appeal for greater price controls had little impact in Washington. The original edition of *Presidential Power*, then, dismissed public politics as ineffective and counterproductive. See Kernell, p. 147 and note 2 on p. 168.

64. To be discussed in greater depth in Chapter 6. I do not intend to suggest that the especially controlled presidential image of the Reagan presidency will be slavishly imitated by all future presidents, but future incumbents will be greatly concerned about protecting and projecting the right image. As television provides a more intimate view of the presidency, presidents will pay greater attention to their image on the evening news. See Chapter 6 of this book, plus Smoller, "The six o'clock Presidency," and Kernell, pp. 73–77 and 85–96.

65. The literature on the president's staff, the Executive Office of the President, OMB, and other aspects of the "Presidential Establishment" (Thomas Cronin's phrase) is voluminous. Some of the most important works in this area are Thomas E. Cronin, "The swelling of the Presidency," *Saturday*

Review 1 (February 1973), pp. 30–36; George Reedy, *The Twilight of the Presidency* (New York: New American Library, 1970); Patrick Anderson, *The President's Men* (Garden City, NY: Doubleday, 1968); Roger Porter, *Presidential Decision-Making: The Economic Policy Board* (New York: Cambridge University Press, 1980); Alexander L. George, *Presidential Decisionmaking in Foreign Policy: The Effective Use of Information and Advice* (Boulder, CO: Westview Press, 1980); John Kessel, "The structures of the Carter White House," *American Journal of Political Science* 27 (August 1983): 431–63; idem., "The Structures of the Reagan White House," *American Journal of Political Science* 28 (May 1984): 231–258; Larry Berman, *The Office of Management and Budget and the Presidency, 1921–1979* (Princeton: Princeton University Press, 1979); Bradley D. Nash, et al., *Organizing and Staffing the Presidency* (New York: Center for the Study of the Presidency, 1980); Harold Seidman and Robert Gilmour, *Politics, Position, and Power*, 4th ed. (New York: Oxford University Press, 1986); Hess, *Organizing the Presidency*; Nathan, *The Administrative Presidency*; and McMurty, *Office of Management and Budget: Evolving Roles and Future Issues.*

66. Evidence of these trends can be seen in the titles of works on the contemporary EOP: Chester A. Newland, "Executive Office policy apparatus: Enforcing the Reagan agenda," in *The Reagan Presidency and the Governing of America*, pp. 135–168; U. S. Congress, House, Committee on Energy and Commerce, *Presidential Control of Agency Rulemaking*, 97th Congress, 1st sess., committee print, 1981; U. S. Congress, Senate, Committee on Environment and Public Works, *Office of Management and Budget Influence on Agency Regulations*; and Terry M. Moe, "The politicized Presidency," in *The New Direction in American Politics*, pp. 235–272.

67. See Berman, op. cit., and McMurty, op. cit.

68. Kessel, "Structures of the Reagan White House," pp. 247–249. Compare the relative importance of OMB in the Eisenhower, Kennedy, Johnson, and even Nixon administrations.

69. Hugh Heclo—"OMB and the Presidency—The problem of 'Neutral Competence'," in *Bureaucratic Power in National Policy Making*, 4th ed., edited by Francis E. Rourke (Boston: Little, Brown, 1986), p. 117—argues correctly that the politicization of OMB has been going on at least since the Kennedy days. As with other trends discussed in this book, however, that politicization has accelerated rapidly in recent years. Moreover, OMB's power vis-à-vis the rest of the Executive Branch has significantly increased; it has emerged into public visibility; and it has entered into the business of lobbying for presidential budget proposals. The OMB of today is not merely the BoB by another name.

70. See Heclo, "Executive budget making," and Schick, "The budget as an instrument of presidential policy."

71. Paul E. Peterson, "The new politics of deficits," in *The New Direction in American Politics*, pp. 365–398. Peterson's article is a good starting point, because there are conflicting estimates on precisely how big the problem is. There is, to my mind, no serious disagreement that there is a long-term problem.

72. See McMurty, pp. 64–71.

73. Much has been written about legislative clearance at OMB, beginning with Neustadt's classic articles in the 1950s. A good summary of the history and current operations of the process can be found in Ronald C. Moe, "Central legislative clearance," in McMurty, *Office of Management and Budget: Evolving Issues and Future Roles*, pp. 169–184.

74. Rosenberg, p. 198.

75. Ibid, p. 199.

76. Ibid., pp. 199–200.

77. I do not intend to suggest that administrative clearance is a panacea for a president's problems with bureaucracy, but neither is it only the creation of a fiendish Ronald Reagan. The lesson of Mr. Reagan's success with it (for his purposes) will not be lost on future presidents.

78. As opposed to a departmental perspective.

79. I. M. Destler, "National Security II: The rise of the assistant (1961–1981)," in *The Illusion of Presidential Government*, pp. 263–285 (Boulder, CO: Westview Press, 1981); Zbigniew Brzezinski, *Power and Principle* (New York: Farrar, Strauss, and Giroux, 1983); Alexander L. George, *Presidential Decisionmaking*; and Robert Hunter, *Presidential Control of Foreign Policy*, The Washington Papers, No. 91 (New York: Praeger and the Center for Strategic and International Studies, Georgetown University, 1982).

80. Until 1969, the bearer of this title was known as the Special Assistant for National Security Affairs. Richard Nixon ended the curious Kennedy-Johnson practice of labelling their senior, permanent, major-issue aides as "special" assistants.

81. Destler, op. cit.

82. See John P. Leacacos, "Kissinger's apparat," *Foreign Policy* 5 (Winter 1971): 3–27.

83. President Reagan's first Assistant for National Security, Richard Allen, was only a minor figure in the Administration. When he departed the government, however, the position was upgraded to one of importance among the handful of senior Reagan aides.

84. By institutionalization, I refer to the development of regularized behavior patterns, complexity, and a seeming permanence. This definition is somewhere between that of Terry Moe in "The politicized Presidency," loc. cit., and Nelson Polsby in "The institutionalization of the U. S. House of Representatives," *American Political Science Review* 62 (March 1968): 144–68. Both of these definitions have merit, but Polsby's is too strict (having been

developed to suit his needs in analyzing Congress), while Moe's is too broad (having been borrowed from sociology and not exactly appropriate for explaining how political structures become institutionalized). I believe that a sense of permanence, even if illusory, is part of what is usually implied by institutionalization.

85. The president is not counted. The units of the contemporary EOP are: Office of the Vice-President (created 1939); The White House Office (1939); OMB (reorganized 1970); Office of Policy Development (with two prior names, 1970); National Security Council (1947); Council of Economic Advisors (1946); Council on Environmental Quality (1969); Office of Science and Technology Policy (1976); Office of Administration (1978); and Office of the U. S. Special Trade Representative (1963). Of the ten units of the EOP that existed in 1968, only six remain. Four new ones have been created, and OMB has undergone enough change since 1970 that it is not the same as the old BoB.

86. Of course, there was much concern about the power of the White House staff in the days of the "imperial" presidency. See, for example, Schlesinger, *The Imperial Presidency*, and Cronin, "The swelling of the Presidency." What is different about this "general secretariat" I am describing is the role of OMB and the "complexification" (if the reader will excuse such a word) of the EOP since 1969. LBJ's White House, famous for the power of aides such as Joe Califano and immortalized by George Reedy's attack in *Twilight of the Presidency*, was quite different from the post-modern presidential establishment: it was less structured, less directly powerful, and smaller.

87. For a discussion of this office in the Reagan Administration, see Mark A. Peterson, "Interest groups and the Reagan White House: For whom the door bell tolls," paper presented to the American Political Science Association, Washington, D. C., 1986.

88. See, for example, Margaret Jane Wyzomirski, "The de-institutionalization of Presidential staff agencies," *Public Administration Review* 42 (September/October 1982): 448–458.

89. See Chester A. Newland, "Executive Office policy apparatus."

90. To use Terry Moe's term.

91. In the Reagan Administration, that capacity has been enhanced by the Cabinet Council system. See Newland, op. cit., and Argyle and Barilleaux, op. cit. Future presidents may not use that system (especially if they are Democrats), so it is not discussed in this survey. Nevertheless, the changes in EOP and OMB in recent years are not likely to be undone by future presidents, regardless of party. President Reagan (and, to some extent, Jimmy Carter before him) has accomplished the White House dominance of Executive Branch policymaking that his predecessors sought.

92. See Samuel Kernell and Samuel L. Popkin, eds., *Chief of Staff: Twenty-Five Years of Managing the Presidency*, (Berkeley, CA: University of California

Press, 1986). The title of this book implies that every president since Eisenhower had a chief of staff. On the contrary, LBJ, JFK, and Carter all opposed such an officer. Carter, of course, later accepted the inevitable. In a discussion of Carter's need for a chief of staff, Dom Bonafede wrote in "The new model year," *National Journal*, November 26, 1977, p. 1859, that Kennedy and Johnson both had staff chiefs (Kenneth O'Donnell and Joe Califano, respectively). That news should come as a surprise to the men chosen to represent those administrations at the University of California, San Diego, conference recorded in *Chief of Staff*: Theodore Sorensen for JFK, and Harry McPherson for LBJ. Indeed, at that conference, Sorensen bluntly denied that JFK ever had a chief of staff. McPherson stated that LBJ had one for only two days, and was not referring to himself. Perhaps the confusion helps to support my contention of a president's need for a clearly defined chief of staff.

93. Attention is usually paid to this point in the matter of Supreme Court justices, but not usually in the less visible positions on independent regulatory commissions. Yet in 1984, the Washington *Post* (January 19, 1984, p. 17) carried a large table showing that President Reagan's regulatory appointees would remain in power for a few years, even if Mr. Reagan was not re-elected.

94. On the expansion of judicial power in U. S. government, see John Agresto, *The Supreme Court and Constitutional Democracy* (Ithaca, NY: Cornell University Press, 1984); Raoul Berger, *Government by Judiciary* (Cambridge, MA: Harvard University Press, 1977); and Richard Neely, *How Courts Govern America* (New Haven, CT: Yale University Press, 1981). On the expansion of administrative regulation, see Ball, op. cit., and Kenneth J. Meier, *Regulation* (New York: St. Martin's, 1985).

95. The best treatment of presidential appointments to the Supreme Court is found in Henry J. Abraham, *Justices and Presidents* (New York: Penguin Books, 1974).

96. Agresto, p. 115.

97. Statement of Allen Schick before the House Committee on Rules, *Legislative Veto After Chadha*, p. 463. The matter of administrative and regulatory power is wrapped up in the debate over the legislative veto since the Supreme Court's ruling in *INS v. Chadha*. The reader is recommended to begin with the hearings volume just cited, which includes testimony from a number of experts, reprints of scholarly articles and court decisions, and an overall thorough survey of the issues involved in the legislative veto debate.

98. P. L. 93–637, officially known as the Federal Trade Commission Improvement Act.

99. Bruce K. Mulock, "Legislative vetoes and the independent regulatory agencies: Whose powers are being balanced and why? *Congressional Research Service Review*, 98th Congress (Fall 1983), reprinted in *Legislative Veto After Chadha*, p. 206.

100. Ibid.

101. Testimony by Norman J. Ornstein, *Legislative Veto After Chadha*, p. 277.

102. The history of executive-congressional relations has never been comprehensively treated in one work. Several important works do, however, illuminate the origins and development of the relations between the branches. See Fisher, *Constititional Conflicts*; McDonald, *The Presidency of George Washington* (Lawrence, KS: University Press of Kansas, 1974); James Sterling Young, *The Washington Community, 1800–1828* (New York: Harcourt, Brace, and World, 1966); James T. Patterson, *Congressional Conservatism in the New Deal* (Lexington: University Press of Kentucky, 1967); Abraham Holtzman, *Legislative Liaison: Executive Leadership in Congress* (Chicago: Rand McNally, 1970); Richard Neustadt, "Presidency and legislation: The growth of central clearance," *American Political Science Review* 48 (Summer 1954): 641–71; Nelson W. Polsby, "Some landmarks in modern Presidential-Congressional relations," in *Both Ends of the Avenue*, pp. 1–25, edited by Anthony King (Washington: American Enterprise Institute, 1983); Eric L. Davis, "Congressional liaison: The people and the institutions," in *Both Ends of the Avenue*, pp. 59–95; Stephen J. Wayne, *The Legislative Presidency* (New York: Harper and Row, 1978); Charles O. Jones, "Congress and the Presidency," in *The New Congress*, pp. 223–49, edited by Thomas Mann and Norman Ornstein (Washington: American Enterprise Institute, 1978); idem., "Presidential negotiations with Congress," in *Both Ends of the Avenue*, pp. 96–130; idem., "Keeping faith and losing congress"; and Stephen J. Wayne, "Congressional liaison in the Reagan White House: A preliminary assessment of the first year," in *President and Congress: Assessing Reagan's First Year*, edited by Norman J. Ornstein (Washington: American Enterprise Institute, 1982), pp. 44–65.

103. See, for example, Evans and Novak, op. cit., on both Eisenhower's and Johnson's relations with Congress.

104. Covered effectively in Leroy N. Rieselbach, *Congressional Reform in the Seventies* (Morristown, NJ: General Learning Press, 1977).

105. For a discussion of the old Congress, see, for example, David W. Rohde, Norman Ornstein, and Robert L. Peabody, "Political change and legislative norms in the U. S. Senate, 1957–1974," in *Studies of Congress*, pp. 147–188, edited by Glenn R. Parker (Washington: Congressional Quarterly Press, 1985); Richard F. Fenno, Jr., "The House Appropriations Committee as a political system: The problem of integration," in *Studies of Congress*, pp. 199–221; and, Randall B. Ripley, "Power in the post-World War II Senate," in *Studies of Congress*, pp. 297–320.

106. Norman Ornstein, "The open Congress meets the President," in *Both Ends of the Avenue*, p. 204.

107. See Jones, "Keeping faith," loc. cit.: and Davis, "Congressional liaison," pp. 75–78.

108. Charles O. Jones has suggested that Ronald Reagan's early successes with Congress are based on that understanding. See his comments as reported in Norman Ornstein, "Introduction," in *President and Congress*, pp. 3–4; and Jones, "Presidential negotiations," p. 126. Anthony King, "A mile and a half is a long way," in *Both Ends of the Avenue*, agrees: "Reagan . . . never served in Congress, but he behaves as though it were his natural metier" (p. 268).

109. Ornstein, "The open Congress meets the President," p. 206.

110. Ibid., p. 205; and idem., "Introduction", loc. cit.

111. The rise of the contemporary vice-presidency has been discussed in a small number of recent works, including J. K. Goldstein, *The Modern American Vice Presidency* (Princeton: Princeton University Press, 1982); Marie D. Natoli, *American Prince, American Pauper* (Westport, CT: Greenwood Press, 1985); Thomas E. Cronin, "Rethinking the Vice-Presidency," in *Rethinking the Presidency*, edited by Thomas E. Cronin (Boston: Little, Brown, 1982); pp. 324–348; and, most notably, Paul C. Light, *Vice-Presidential Power* (Baltimore: Johns Hopkins University Press, 1984). Light's book has gained the most attention of all these works. He is enthusiastic about the new prominence of the second office in the nation, while Cronin remains more sober. I find Light's enthusiasm infectious, but think that Cronin's attitude is a needed counterweight.

112. My discussion of the new vice-presidency draws heavily on the work of Light, but the interpretation of how it fits into the post-modern presidency is my own.

113. Both Mondale and Bush were important guides for their presidents to the workings of Congress. Moreover, each came to the vice-presidency with a substantial background that qualified him to offer advice of value to his president. See Light, part II.

114. The Office of the Vice-President (OVP) now resembles the EOP White House Office in microcosm. This is a far cry from the days when Hubert Humphrey had to hide his former Senate aides on the staffs of the various commissions Humphrey chaired. For a look at the OVP, see the current issue of the *U. S. Government Manual*. An organizational diagram of OVP (circa 1974) was published in *National Journal* and is reprinted in Light, p. 273.

115. Little sustained attention has been devoted to the issue of presidential succession. For a thoughtful introduction to the topic, see Aaron Wildavsky, "Presidential succession and disability: Policy analysis for unique cases," in *The Presidency*, pp. 777–795.

116. President Reagan's temporary transfer of power to Vice-President Bush while undergoing surgery in 1985 illustrates this problem: if we cannot have an unconcious president for even a few hours (due to nuclear weapons, etc.), how can we expect to turn power over to a cypher?

117. In the 1960s, the Senate was thought to be the breeding ground for future presidents. In the 1980s, many major figures in the presidential contest

have been officials with little or no experience in Washington (e. g., Mario Cuomo, Bruce Babbitt, Chuck Robb, Pierre du Pont, Thomas Kean, and, of course, Jimmy Carter and Ronald Reagan).

118. See Evans and Novak, op. cit.

2

The Rise and Fall of the Modern Presidency

Franklin Roosevelt cast a long shadow on American politics. His New Deal altered the direction of public policy; his legislative initiatives permanently changed the role of the federal government in the life of the nation; and, his tenure transformed forever the office he held for twelve years. After FDR, there was no turning back to the old American order.

The office of the presidency was particularly affected by his incumbency. Indeed, what is usually called the modern presidency was to a large extent the Rooseveltian presidency. FDR was a prototype for his successors in office, many of whom attempted to emulate his imprint on the government.[1]

But the modern presidency is now a thing of the past, for the contemporary office is post-modern in nature. It is no longer the extension of FDR into the future, but has been transformed into something substantively different. As the preceding chapter has outlined, the shape of the post-modern presidency was recently formed.

Why has this transformation occurred? There are two fundamental reasons: 1) through a series of events and trends that culminated in Watergate and the end of the Vietnam War, the modern presidency, as it had been understood, was brought down; and, 2) by the 1980s, a number of developments had altered the nature of the presidency suf-

ficiently to mark a new phase in the evolution of the office. Many of
the developments that created the post-modern presidency existed
throughout the modern period of the office, but it was in their fulfillment
that the change occurred.

Because the post-modern presidency is a variation on the previous
phase, it is necessary to understand the modern presidency in order to
appreciate the changes that have occurred. Only then is the distinctive-
ness of the post-modern presidency apparent.

The story is best told thematically, because it condenses half a century
of history into a few pages. In the rise and fall of the modern presidency
lie the origins of the contemporary presidency.

THE RISE OF THE MODERN PRESIDENCY

While Franklin Roosevelt was the father of the modern presidency,
he did not create that office from nothing. Rather, he built on precedents
and trends that existed before his time, and added his own ideas to
adapt the office to his own needs and the circumstances of his time.
The result was that the traditional presidency was left behind.[2]

Yet, that traditional presidency was not insignificant. It had demonstrated the potential for presidential autonomy and leadership, as in
the cases of Washington, Jackson, Lincoln, Teddy Roosevelt, and Wilson. What separated the old from the new was that presidential activism
would now be a fixture of American government. In the traditional
understanding of the office, presidential assertiveness was not a permanent feature of American politics.

The Traditional Presidency

Before the rise of the modern presidency, the Chief Executive was
not expected always to be the driving force in the government. Despite
Hamilton's insistence in *The Federalist*, No. 70, that "Energy in the
executive is a leading character in the definition of good government,"[3]
presidential activism was not the rule for much of U. S. history.

Except for foreign affairs, the leading role in defining national policy
was generally left to Congress. Presidents contributed their suggestions
and took some interest in legislation, but there was nothing like a
presidential legislative program.

Nor did presidents have much staff support. Administration was left largely to the Cabinet departments, which served the legislature as well as the Chief Executive. The president worked out of his living room or a study, borrowing secretarial help from his family or the departments.

Unilateral presidential actions certainly occurred, whether because of presidential inclination (Jackson, T. Roosevelt) or national necessity (Jefferson and the Louisiana Purchase, Lincoln and the Civil War), but they were not perceived as conventional presidential behavior. Indeed, Rexford Tugwell,[4] a student of the development of the office, has characterized the guiding principle of the traditional presidency as the "Rule of Restraint."[5] According to this rule, unless some great public necessity demanded assertiveness by the president, he was obliged to restrain himself as befit a republican chief of state. The president was not supposed to enlarge his powers, but hold them in reserve until circumstances demanded otherwise.

When the times so demanded, observed Tugwell, the president was to be guided by the "Rule of Necessity."[6] According to this rule, the president was obliged to act in whatever fashion was necessary to protect the national interest. In the period of the traditional presidency, such occasions were rare.

As a result, many of the traditional presidents were minor figures in U. S. history. Presidents such as Millard Filmore and Warren Harding have been remembered humorously, or appear more frequently in parlor trivia games than in the pages of American history books.

Of course, not all traditional presidents were so unmemorable. Most of America's great presidential heroes were men of this period: Washington, Jefferson, and Lincoln, if only to name the three enshrined in the nation's capital. The forceful actions of some traditional Chief Executives set important precedents for their successors, from the Louisiana Purchase to conduct of the Civil War to trust-busting.

Even in the midst of the traditional presidency, however, there were glimmers of change. First, the twentieth century brought with it an expanding role for the United States in world politics. That expansion manifest itself to some degree in greater presidential power in foreign affairs. Theodore Roosevelt and Woodrow Wilson were international figures in their time, each in his own way foreshadowing the presidential role of "World Leader" that would appear because of World War II.

Second, the foundations of future presidential dominance over the Executive Branch policymaking were laid in the time of Coolidge and Hoover. The Budget and Accounting Act of 1921 created not only the

Bureau of the Budget (which would grow up to be OMB), but also the presidential budget. Here was the earliest beginning of the end for departmental autonomy in budgeting.[7] President Hoover would expand presidential control over the departments as he attempted cope with the Great Depression.

Third, the role of president as chief legislator, which would be secured by FDR, has roots as old as the republic. The Washington-Hamilton financial program not only occupied much of the attention of the First Congress, but it also effectively created the American economic system.[8] Jefferson took an active role in legislative affairs while in the White House, as did Theodore Roosevelt. Finally, Woodrow Wilson came to the office with his New Freedom program, which served as a set of legislative initiatives.

These precedents would be used and built upon by FDR, who moved the presidency into a whole new kind of existence. The president now became the center of the government, replacing Congress as the focus of policymaking and representation. As Tugwell put it, a new rule of presidential behavior now took effect: the "Rule of Responsibility."[9] It overrode and made obsolete the two rules of the traditional presidency. According to this rule, it became the responsibility of the president to "grasp and project what is necessary to secure the nation's future."[10] Once this concept of the presidency gained currency, the traditional presidency ceased to exist.

The Development of the Modern Presidency

In order to deal with the problems of the Great Depression, FDR felt compelled not only to transform the role of the federal government in the life of the nation, but to revolutionize the role of the president both within the national government and in the American mind. The presidency now became the center of politics and the center of attention.

What was the nature of this transformation? Fred Greenstein has described it succinctly in four points that summarize some of the most important changes:[11]

(1) From a state of affairs in which there was at best a somewhat grudging acceptance that the President would be "interested" in the doings of Congress, it has come to be taken for granted that he *should* regularly initiate and seek to win support for legislative action as part of his continuing responsibilities.

The President has come to be far more active in evaluating legislative enactments with a view to deciding whether to exercise the veto than traditionally was the case.

This change, of course, was the most important aspect of the modern presidency. The hallmark of a modern president was his legislative program, and observers focused their attention on the Chief Legislator's use of the "power to persuade" Congress to adopt that program. Indeed, for many years, *Congressional Quarterly* tracked each president's "box-score" to measure his level of success at persuasion.[12]

Other presidential activities were considered important, but subsidiary to this task. After all, it was reasoned, only the president represents the national interest, so he must be the source of policy. Even budget making, which was coming more and more to determine the actual shape of government policy, was not accorded the same respect as legislative initiatives. President Eisenhower's attention to the budget during his tenure was criticized as anachronistic, despite its role in shaping defense and social policy in the 1950s. Modern presidents were supposed to initiate new laws and programs first.

(2) From a presidency that normally exercised few unilateral powers, there has been a shift to one that is provided—via statutes, court decisions, and informal precedents—with many more occasions for direct policy making through executive orders and other actions not formally ratified by Congress.

In this regard, the most significant presidential policymaking was in foreign affairs. U. S. intervention in Korea and Indochina occurred through presidential war making, a controversial concept that was never quite repudiated even as it was made more politically difficult in the 1970s.[13]

But presidents also expanded their powers in other areas. Executive Orders ended segregation in the armed forces, required affirmative action by builders to hire minority workers for federal construction projects, and impounded funds appropriated by Congress. In addition, the Chief Executive acquired such economic powers as the ability to impose wage-price controls and negotiate tariff reductions. Overall, the policymaking power of the presidency expanded.

(3) From a presidency with extremely modest staff support, there has evolved one in which the President has at his disposal in the Executive Office and "on

loan'' from elsewhere in the executive branch an extensive bureaucracy to implement his initiatives. It is only because of the rise of a presidential bureaucracy that it has been possible for Presidents to follow through on (1) and (2).

This third point is essential for understanding the development of the modern presidency, for it reveals an important trend: the growth and institutionalization of agencies intended to support the presidential office. Later developments of these agencies take on significance only in contrast to that institutionalization.

Following the creation of the Executive Office of the President in 1939, there occurred four decades of presidential agency growth. The size and number of EOP units increased, and the total number of staff positions expanded steadily. A key aspect of that growth was the institutionalization of these agencies: they grew larger, more complex, more permanent, and distinct from the presidency itself. The overall growth of the EOP was called the ''swelling of the presidency'' or the ''institutionalization of the presidency,'' but in truth it was not exactly that. Rather, the development of the EOP before about 1970 was in reality the institutionalization of bureaucratic units distinct from the president and his immediate political staff.[14] OMB in particular developed along lines stressing neutral competence, long tenure and low turnover of staff, and an overall commitment to professionalism.[15]

The response of presidents and their political aides to that institutionalization was a series of attempts to control and/or circumvent these agencies, but to little avail.[16] It would not be until the 1970s and 1980s that the politicization of OMB and other units would advance sufficiently to satisfy the presidents involved. So, the general character of the EOP in the period of the modern presidency was one of increasing complexity and permanence, but torn between the competing demands of professionalism and political utility to the president.

Throughout the modern period, most presidents (especially Democrats) emulated FDR's loose style of management. Despite the expansion and growing complexity of the EOP, the ideal of the president as his own chief of staff remained a standard for assessing the competence of the Chief Executive.[17] The politician who was to be Chief Legislator and national leader was not to have a senior assistant stand between him and the levers of power.

(4) Finally, there appear to have been major changes in the quantity and quality of public attention to incumbent Presidents. For many Americans the complex, uncertain political world of our times seems to be dealt with by personification, in the form of perceptions of the quality of performance and personal virtue of the incumbent President. Presidents are expected to be symbols of reassurance, possessing extraordinary "nonpolitical" personal qualities that traditionally were associated only with long deceased "hero presidents" of the past, such as George Washington. At the same time they are expected to be politically effective, bringing about favorable national and international social conditions. They have become the beneficiaries of anything positive that can be attributed to the government, but also scapegoats for social and political discontent.

The upshot of this change was that the political system came to be seen as revolving around the president. Expectations of government were visited upon the incumbent president, so the man in office became the focus of national politics. More and more attention was paid to the every move and word of the president, from major actions to routine physical examinations.

A concomitant change was the increasing journalistic attention to the presidency. With the advent of television, voters could see the president directly and be reached by him. The media found a new focus on incumbents and candidates that helped to intensify the personalization of politics.

The Environment of the Modern Presidency

The modern presidency did not exist in a vacuum, however. It was intimately associated with a political environment that consisted of particular institutional arrangements and policy issues.

One important feature of that environment was the association of the modern presidency with governmental activism and the liberal agenda. The modern presidency and the "positive state" of the New Deal/Great Society consensus were inextricably linked.[18] The presidency was described by its admirers as the only institution in the government with a "national" perspective and constituency, because Congress was too "parochial" in outlook.

This interpretation led many observers to evaluate presidents in terms of their support for and advancement of governmental activism. Thomas Cronin would later call this view the "textbook presidency," because it came to be represented in all of the major American government texts of the 1950s and 1960s:[19]

> With the New Deal presidency in mind, these textbooks portrayed the president instructing the nation as a national teacher and guiding the nation as national preacher. Presidents, they said, should expand the role of the federal government to cope with the increasing nationwide demands for social justice and a prosperous economy. . . .

Textbooks do no more or less than reflect the conventional academic wisdom of their time, so Cronin's analysis serves as good evidence of the link between the modern presidency and the liberal agenda. Nor did the two conservative presidents of the modern period, Eisenhower and Nixon, break that link: Eisenhower left the New Deal intact, while Nixon challenged only peripheral aspects (e.g., the Office of Economic Opportunity) of the Great Society Programs.

A second aspect of the political environment was its institutional structure. Even with the growing power of courts and regulatory agencies in the middle of the twentieth century, government in the age of the modern presidency was still conducted mostly by the president and Congress. The process of making and implementing public policy was still dominated by presidential-congressional bargaining. Regulatory and judicial institutions had not yet gained the power they would later achieve, so presidential appointments in those areas had not yet assumed the significance they would come to acquire.

Congress in this period was still "clubby" in nature. Power was distributed through the seniority system, and resided largely in the committee chairmen. These "barons," mostly Southern Democrats, were generally insulated from constituent pressures and free to bargain with the president.[20] The result of these structures was that interactions between the president and powerful Members of Congress largely shaped national policy.

Finally, the modern presidency operated amidst the politics of the unreformed electoral system. American political parties were greatly decentralized, with greatest influence residing in state and local party organizations.[21] Even with the growing influence of primaries in the nominating system during the 1960s, presidential candidate selection in the modern period was generally controlled by party professionals ("bosses") in state and local organizations.

The political environment of the modern presidency, then, could be characterized as one of "elite bargaining."[22] Bargaining among party and interest group elites determined nominations. Presidents governed largely through bargaining with congressional and major interest group elites. Kernell terms this situation "institutionalized pluralism," because it contained a heterogeneous but nevertheless limited number of relatively stable interests and components. Therefore, Neustadt's prescription of a "bargaining president" to operate in this environment, for all its shortcomings, was a logical response to the circumstances of the time.[23] Now at the center of politics and the center of attention, the president had to be a successful bargainer in order to live up to the demands of his office.

THE CLIMAX OF THE MODERN PRESIDENCY

The Nixon Administration represents the climax of the modern presidency. Richard Nixon both fulfilled several trends apparent in the evolving office, and initiated changes in it. In Watergate and his conduct of the Vietnam War, he also stimulated a backlash against president-dominated government. Finally, his tenure in office occurred during a time of important changes in the political environment.

President Nixon fulfilled several trends of the modern presidency. He secured presidential dominance over policymaking, particularly in foreign affairs. The State Department lost nearly all influence, as the president and his National Security Advisor ran the Vietnam War and high-level diplomacy from the White House.[24] The trend toward president-centered government reached its height during these years.

The White House staff grew much larger and more complex, as a natural consequence of the centralization of power there. A miniature State Department was created in the staff of the National Security Council, and other White House units took on administrative functions previously held by line agencies. Critics labelled the staff a "palace guard" and decried the "imperial presidency," but Nixon was largely continuing in the tradition of FDR, Kennedy, and Johnson.

The fulfillment of at least one trend had the effect of inaugurated a change in the presidency. Nixon's transformation of the BoB into OMB, achieving the expansion of EOP influence that other presidents had sought, laid the foundation for the development of what would become the president's "general secretariat." The new OMB gained the power of limited regulatory clearance, in the Quality of Life Review process,[25] setting the stage for the eventual consolidation of administrative clearance in the post-modern presidency. Political Assistant Directors (PADs) were installed in OMB between the Director and the professional career staff, thus accelerating the politicization of the agency that had been going on for a number of years. At the same time, the Director became a White House assistant, foreshadowing the central political role that position would eventually come to play (under David Stockman).

In short, the creation of OMB in 1970 marked both an end and a beginning. It fulfilled the trend of politicization that had begun in 1939, when Bob was transferred to EOP from the Treasury, and in doing so ended neutral competence as a distinguishing characteristic of the agency. Thus began the development of the president's "general secretariat."

Moreover, President Nixon initiated other changes in the office that heralded the beginning of a new phase in the development of the presidency. He began the recent trend of "going public" that was discussed in Chapter 1, appearing frequently on television and even timing political events to coincide with prime-time evening viewing. He was trying to reach past Congress and the press to the public, because of his conviction that only in doing so could he reach the "silent majority" of Americans who supported his goals.

The Nixon presidency also marked the enlargement of presidential budgetary powers and the growing importance of the budget as an instrument for governing. The president used his power to impound funds appropriated by Congress, in order to halt spending on programs he did not want. This action ultimately stimulated Congress to halt the practice in the Budget and Impoundment Act of 1974. He also used OMB to shape departmental budget requests, in order to control the growth of government through budgeting rather than legislation. Unlike impoundment, the increasing centralization of executive budgeting would be a lasting feature of presidential policymaking.

Nixon's success at running the government his way, plus the political disaster of Watergate, induced a backlash against president-dominated government. Congress began a resurgence after the 1972 election, but the backlash gained momentum after the 1974 congressional elections brought in a large class of new members eager for change.[26] A slate of presidency-curbing legislation was passed into law, some of it even over Nixon's veto:[27] the requirement that the OMB director receive Senate confirmation for appointment (1973); the Impoundment Control Act of 1974; the Case Act (1972); and the War Powers Resolution (1973).

During this time, the political environment also was in flux. The decade of the 1960s and opposition to the Vietnam War induced a number of changes in U. S. politics. The "clubby" Congress would soon be gone, replaced by the "open" Congress of the late 1970s and afterward. The political agenda was changing, just as was the electoral system and the balance of political power in the government. All of these changes, along with the collapse of the Nixon Administration, would contribute to the fall of the modern presidency.

THE DECLINE OF THE MODERN PRESIDENCY

Like the fall of the Roman empire, the decline of the modern presidency was a protracted process. As with all other transitions in history, the end of one order was entangled with the birth of the next.

The decade of the 1970s was a period of transformation, as the presidency and its political environment underwent a series of changes. By the later years of that decade, observers were trying to describe and groping to explain the developments of the previous decade. One prominent book of the period, *The New American Political System* (1978),[28] contained essays by a number of experts seeking to make sense of all that had happened. The clear implication of their works was that changes had indeed occurred, both in the institutions of government and in the larger political environment.

What was not so easily detected, because it was not yet sufficiently developed, was the transition from the modern to the post-modern presidency.[29] That transition would not become apparent until several years afterward, but it was in progress even as *The New American Political System* was in press.

The Changing Political Environment

The 1970s brought a number of changes in the American political environment, both in the issues of the day and in the structure of politics. These changes would influence the operations and even the nature of the presidency.

The issue structure of American politics changed in the 1970s, as a new political agenda began to take shape. This new agenda was a consolidative one, questioning government expansion and stressing the need to control inflation, bureaucracy, and the overall cost of government. Since the liberal agenda, with a few important exceptions,[30] had been largely enacted, the New Deal/Great Society consensus ran out of steam and began to break down. Now, the rising issues were ones that often cut across the lines that had marked American politics for forty-odd years: budgetary restraint, inflation, taxes, energy, the environment, social issues (abortion, women's rights, pornography, etc.), "big government," and other topics not associated with traditional politics.

This new agenda coincided with the institutional shift from the positive state to the regulatory state.[31] The old issue consensus had supported the "positive state" of welfare, education, and social programs. In the new issue age, regulation was increasingly the order of the day. The power of regulatory agencies expanded in the 1970s, as did the role of courts in regulating national domestic and social policy.[32] Consequently, not only was the liberal agenda traditionally associated withthe modern presidency passing away, but significant policymaking power was shifting to administrative and judicial bodies.

In the institutional domain of presidential-congressional relations, attention was becoming focused more and more on budgetary issues. Richard Nixon had done battle with Congress over the budget, but in defeat had turned to impoundment and lost that battle as well. Gerald Ford tried to restrain spending in his battle against inflation, but lacked an electoral base with which to take on the resurgent Congress. So he relied on a veto strategy to stop spending, albeit with poor results. When Jimmy Carter entered the White House, he pledged a balanced budget by the end of his first term. Congress still enacted legislation, but the annual cycle of budget making in the reformed budget process had come to constitute the most important device for setting national policy.[33]

Changes in budgeting were only part of a larger set of alterations in the legislative branch. The reforms of the 1970s transformed the "clubby" Congress into an open institution of fragmented power and decentralization.[34] It was now served by a large professional staff organization that enabled members to compete with the president in policymaking.[35]

These changes were accompanied by electoral reforms that opened the presidential nominating system to party activists. The use of primaries for selecting delegates expanded, and the presidential campaign season grew longer for each election.[36] The election of Jimmy Carter, who took advantage of the new system to gain the nomination over several Washington "insiders," seemed to symbolize the extent of changes in the nominating system.[37]

Finally, Watergate had intensified a trend begun with the rise of television, and one that continued well after Richard Nixon left office: the growth in the influence of the press in American politics. Just as presidents were now always in the public eye, the media was devoting more attention to the Chief Executive. Moreover, that attention was not strictly neutral, but investigative and often adversarial in nature.[38] Presidents were now going public more often, and when they were not the press was going after the president.

In sum, the political environment emerging in the 1970s was different than the one that had characterized the previous decade. American politics was not what it had been, nor was the presidency.

The Ford–Carter Interregnum

The 1970s marked a low point for the presidency. President Nixon left office in disgrace in 1974, and two years later his successor was defeated in his bid to gain the office by election. Jimmy Carter followed with a presidency wracked with troubles. Soon, he was also defeated in his reelection bid.

Observers of this string of defeats expressed grave doubts about the future of the presidency. Soon, the term "post-imperial" presidency became current. It seemed to capture the sense that the very executive institution was in decline, and a host of learned and journalistic works were written to describe and explain that fall.

Writers on the presidency in the 1970s wrung their hands over the fate of the office, as they explained the conditions that made it "impossible," "intractable," or just powerless.[39] Gerald Ford's reliance on the veto to make budget policy, and then his subsequent defeat in 1976, were taken as signs of an office in trouble. When Jimmy Carter, declining in the opinion polls and unable to move Congress, blamed his problems on a "national malaise," these writers saw the office in a tailspin. When Carter lost his race for a second term, many worried out loud about the stability of American government.

These concerns sprang from two sources. First, many analysts were nostalgic for the days of the New Deal, the New Frontier, and the Great Society. Rather than budgetary restraint and lower expectations, they wanted a politics of expansion and new initiatives. But a second factor was also important: short-sightedness.

The diagnoses of an ''impossible'' or ''no-win'' presidency were built on the assumption that the weaknesses of the Ford and Carter presidencies were systemic. Taking a short-run problem as chronic disability,[40] these writers argued that the future of the presidency would be a troubled one.

Because of this short-sighted focus on weakness, many trends of change afoot during this period went unnoticed or underestimated. The rise of OMB within the government, the centralization of budget making in the White House, the institutionalization of the presidency rather than EOP units, and the greater tendency of presidents to go public, all received insufficient attention or were misunderstood. The presidency was assumed to be in trouble and nothing else was as important.

In retrospect, however, these changes were some of the most important features of the period. American government and politics were in flux, and the Ford-Carter period was a sort of interregnum between the modern and post-modern presidencies.

Ronald Reagan and the Renascent Presidency

The epilogue to the story is the Reagan presidency. It showed how time-bound the diagnoses and analyses of the 1970s had been, as Ronald Reagan won stunning budget victories in 1981 and demonstrated presidential forcefulness once again.

Mr. Reagan consolidated many of the changes underway before his coming and also made his own contributions to the evolving presidency. He made permanent the changes in the political agenda. He installed a chief of staff to manage his ''general secretariat,'' gave his vice-president a significant role in the administration, and advanced the cause of governing through public politics. In addition, the president and his OMB Director imposed a ''top-down'' budgeting system, which enabled them to revolutionize the whole process of fiscal policymaking. Mr. Reagan even ran up ''conservative'' deficits in his budgets—that is, deficits to pay for defense and lower taxes.

Yet, with the problems he encountered in the Iran-Contra scandal, Mr. Reagan illustrated the fragility of an individual president's influence. That scandal weakened his presidency in its last two years, because it mired the Reagan Administration in a controversy over the president's competence and ability to keep his own house in order.

Nevertheless, the Iran-Contra scandal did not alter the nature of the changes that had occurred since the decline of the modern presidency. If the scandal had erupted early in the Reagan years, it might have aborted some of the developments of the past two decades. By coming at the end of the Reagan presidency, however, the scandal concentrated its damage on Mr. Reagan and his staff. The trends that characterize the post-modern presidency remained intact.

The upshot of these developments was that the post-modern presidency had now arrived. It had been taking shape for so long, but was now in place. Presidents after Mr. Reagan would be sure to occupy a different position than the one assumed by the modern presidents from the 1940s to the 1960s.

NOTES

1. FDR's legacy for his successors was a comparison of each incumbent with observers' idealized memories of the man from Hyde Park. The burden has been great, but I would not go so far as William Leuchtenburg has in his book, which claims that each successive president has labored to live up to FDR's image. In order to make his point, Leuchtenburg must stretch things a bit, interpreting the behavior of every president as if that man compared everything about himself with FDR. See William Leuchtenburg, *In the Shadow of FDR* (Ithaca, NY: Cornell University Press, 1983).

2. The term "traditional presidency" is Fred Greenstein's, used in the two essays he wrote on the evolution of the office. See Fred Greenstein, Larry Berman, and Alvin S. Felzenberg, with Doris Lidtke, *Evolution of the Modern Presidency: A Bibliographic Survey* (Washington: American Enterprise Institute, 1977), pp. i-ix; and Greenstein, "Change and continuity," loc. cit.

3. Alexander Hamilton, James Madison, and John Jay, *The Federalist Papers*, with an introduction by Clinton Rossiter (New York: New American Library, 1961), p. 423.

4. Tugwell was a member of FDR's "brain trust" and the appointed governor of Puerto Rico.

5. Rexford G. Tugwell, *The Enlargement of the Presidency* (New York: Doubleday, 1960). Tugwell has written the best history of the presidency, but, unfortunately, it stops during the Eisenhower years.

6. Ibid.

7. For a discussion of the Act and of its offspring, see Berman, *The Office*

of Management and Budget and the Presidency, pp. 3–15. See also McMurty, *Office of Management and Budget: Evolving Roles and Future Issues.*

8. Forrest McDonald, *The Presidency of George Washington* (Lawrence, KS: University Press of Kansas, 1974).

9. Tugwell, p. 348.

10. Ibid., p. 348.

11. Greenstein, "Change and continuity," pp. 45–46. The following section draws heavily on that essay and Greenstein, et al., *Evolution*, pp. iii-vii. Any interpretations of trends and developments that are inconsistent or at odds with Professor Greenstein's analysis are my own.

12. See *Congressional Quarterly Almanac* for the years before 1975.

13. Presidential war making was in effect legitimated by the War Powers Resolution, because that law recognized the president's right to commit troops without prior congressional approval. See Fisher, *Constitutional Conflicts*; Franck and Weisband; and, Franklin, op. cit.

14. Wyzomirski, op. cit., essentially makes this point in reverse, when she argues that the politicization of OMB, NSC, etc., means the de-institutionalization of those agencies/staffs. If bringing agencies under greater political control by the president is de-institutionalization, then institutionalization must mean growing more distinct from the president.

15. Ibid., pp. 457–458.

16. See Heclo, "OMB and the President," loc. cit.

17. For a discussion of this point, see James P. Pfiffner, "White House Staff versus the Cabinet: Centripetal and centrifugal roles," *Presidential Studies Quarterly* 16 (Fall 1986): 666–690, especially the Neustadt quote on p. 668.

18. This point has been made or corroborated in a number of places. See Greenstein, "Change and continuity", pp. 65–67, and Karen J. Winkler, "Experts voice second thoughts about the virtues of a strong Presidency," *The Chronicle of Higher Education* (September 17, 1986), pp. 1 and 8.

19. Thomas E. Cronin, *The State of the Presidency*, 2nd ed. (Boston: Little, Brown, 1980), p. 78.

20. See Ornstein, "The open Congress," pp. 189–195, and Kernell, pp. 10–13.

21. For a discussion of the "old" (i.e., pre–1968) party system, see James W. Ceasar, *Presidential Selection* (Princeton: Princeton University Press, 1979), pp. 213–303; Xandra Kayden and Eddie Mahe, Jr., *The Party Goes On* (New York: Basic Books, 1985), pp. 1–56; and William Crotty and John S. Jackson III, *Presidential Primaries and Nominations* (Washington: Congressional Quarterly Press, 1985), pp. 7–24.

22. Crotty and Jackson, loc. cit. Crotty and Jackson use this term to describe the nominating system only, but it is also applicable to governing.

23. As perceptive as Neustadt's analysis was, it suffered from some serious

problems. See, for example, Sperlich, op. cit., and Michael Nelson, "Two steps forward (is) one step back: Post-Neustadtian Presidential scholarship," *Presidency Research* 7 (Spring 1985): 22–27.

24. The literature on the Nixon presidency is voluminous. A good place to start is William Safire, *Before the Fall* (New York: Belmont Tower Books, 1975). Safire is not unbiased, having been a speechwriter for President Nixon, but his memoir is neither uncritical nor uninformative.

25. See Chapter 1 of this book, and Ball, op. cit.

26. Detailed in Riselbach, op. cit.

27. The term "presidency-curbing legislation" is Fred Greenstein's.

28. Anthony King, ed., *The New American Political System* (Washington: American Enterprise Institute, 1978).

29. In this comment I do not mean to cast any aspersions on Fred Greenstein's essay in that volume, "Change and continuity. . . . " Professor Greenstein's article was an enlightening summary of the development of the presidency through the 1970s. But it is limited by the view, which was essentially universal during the Carter years, that the presidency was mired in the "intractable" (to use Greenstein's term) politics of the post-Watergate era. Soon, Mr. Reagan would take over and dispel most of this thinking.

30. Charles Jones has made a similar observation. See his "Keeping faith," pp. 441–442.

31. Most notably, national health insurance and the Equal Rights Amendment. Otherwise, the liberals had gotten just about everything they had wanted.

32. The expression "from the positive to the regulatory state" is the subtitle of Seidman and Gilmour's *Politics, Position, and Power*.

33. See Chapter 1, section on "Vicarious Policymaking."

34. Discussed in Allan Schick, *Congress and Money* (Washington: Urban Institute Press, 1980).

35. See Chapter 3 on the new Congress.

36. Of course, Congress did not develop any capacity for an independent legislative program, but its newly expanded staffs enabled members to initiate legislation and to challenge presidential proposals.

37. Reforms in the presidential nominating system are discussed in Ceasar, *Presidential Selection*; idem., *Reforming the Reforms* (Washington: Ballinger, 1982); Crotty and Jackson, Presidential Primaries and Nominations; and Nelson Polsby, *Consequences of Party Reform* (New York: Oxford University Press, 1983). These works are representative rather than exhaustive: the literature on the reforms in the nominating system is extensive, and much of it is repetitive.

38. Carter, of course, also took advantage of the anti-Watergate mood in the country. But his nomination and election were possible only because of the reformed electoral system.

39. The bible of investigative journalism was by Carl Bernstein and Bob

Woodward, *All the President's Men* (New York: Simon Schuster, 1974), which is about its two authors as much as it is about Watergate. The self-consciously intense activist journalist now found throughout the profession is a consequence of the self-promotion of Woodward and Bernstein.

40. Everyone in this period seemed to have a better explanation for the decline of the presidency and a more pessimistic view of its future. Two excellent representatives of this literature are Joseph Kraft, ''The post-imperial Presidency,'' loc. cit.; and Godfrey Hodgson, *All Things to All Men: The False Promise of the Modern American Presidency* (New York: Simon and Schuster, 1980).

3

The New
Political
Environment

Not only is the post-modern presidency distinctive in itself, but it exists in an environment different from the one surrounding its predecessors. This new political environment provides the context for governance in the post-modern era.

The political environment is the sum of issues, interests, and institutions that frame the politics of a particular time, and it has changed in recent years. With the many upheavals occurring in the United States over the past two decades, the very shape of national politics has been altered. The nation has entered a period marked by individualized politics, fiscal stress, institutional change, and the shift of significant political power toward unelected officials in the bureaucracy and the judiciary. The days of governmental expansiveness and the "positive state" have given way to fiscal restraint and regulation.

This new environment developed over a number of years, just as the post-modern presidency evolved over time. It was not created by Ronald Reagan alone, although he helped to give it form.

As the product both of Reagan's actions and of larger trends, the new political environment provides the context for presidential politics in the late twentieth century. It consists of several elements, not all of equal importance, that combine to make contemporary American politics distinctive: 1) the new political agenda; 2) the budget as the central instrument for governing; 3) the new electoral politics; 4) the media age; 5) the new Congress; and, 6) policymaking by administrative and judicial bodies.

THE NEW POLITICAL AGENDA

The agenda of major national political issues is never static, but one can identify different periods in the overall shape of that agenda. From the Great Depression through the 1960s, the agenda was marked by the issues that characterized the New Deal and Great Society: welfare, education, civil rights, and general governmental activism in the "positive state." Since the late 1960s, however, there has been a shift in the national political issue structure. As Charles Robb, former Democratic governor of Virginia, put it, "The political era that was dominated by the New Deal and everything that has flowed from it has run its course."[1]

In the new political agenda, the issues are restraint and consolidation of governmental programs, regulation versus deregulation of business, arms control and the future of defense, and dealing with fiscal stress. These were not the concerns of the "positive state."

This new issue structure is the product of three developments in U. S. politics. The first is the general success of the liberal agenda. As defined by the New Deal and Great Society programs, the issues that marked American politics for three decades were largely settled. The federal government achieved a dominant role in national political life, offering a broad range of services and managing the national economy. Civil rights and other equal protection laws were passed to end traditional forms of discrimination. On the whole, the goals generally associated with the Democratic Party and liberal activists were achieved.

The result of that success was to make room for new issues. But it also drew attention to questions of efficiency and effectiveness in managing the programs already enacted. Concerns about governmental waste and "big government" replaced expansion and activism. Four presidents in succession, from Nixon to Reagan, made these concerns their targets.[2]

The second development was the structural change from the "positive state" to the "regulatory state." During the 1960s and 1970s, regulation came to play an increasingly important role in government. Following the creation of the Environmental Protection Agency and the expansion of the powers of such regulatory bodies as the Federal Trade Commission, the term "regulatory state" became an increasingly appropriate label for characterizing American government. Moreover, the growing tendency of Congress to pass general laws and assign to executive departments the power to implement them through published rules meant that many substantive policy decisions were being made in the bureaucracy. Everything from the environment to medical school admissions to consumer products were regulated in some fashion.[3]

The result, of course, was a heated debate about the relative merits of regulation as a means for promoting national goals. This debate did not fit the traditional liberal-conservative split in politics, for the coalitions supporting or attacking specific kinds of regulation were often unusual. Airline deregulation, for example, passed into law at the behest of a liberal Democrat (Sen. Ted Kennedy) and a conservative Republican (Rep. Phil Crane). Consequently, it distinguished contemporary policy battles from earlier ones.

Presidents have entered into these battles, particularly in their attempts to control rulemaking by executive branch agencies.[4] The post-modern presidency's power of administrative clearance is a response to the rise of the "regulatory state."

Finally, fiscal stress is a third development that shapes the new political agenda. While the expansiveness of the 1960s gave way to fiscal restraint in the 1970s, the 1980s brought a new condition of fiscal stress. Ronald Reagan came to the presidency determined to reshape the nation's fiscal program: he wanted to cut domestic spending, increase defense spending, and reduce taxes.[5] Congress gave him much of what he wanted, but not all of it. For example, it would not give him the deep domestic cuts he wanted.[6]

The result was the establishment of a long-term deficit problem for the United States.[7] By fiscal 1986, the budget deficit had reached a record $220.7 billion.[8] In the first five years of the Reagan Administration, the national debt expanded from 27 to 42 percent of the gross national product (GNP).[9] Budget making for the foreseeable future would occur under this condition of fiscal stress: there would not be enough revenue to cover existing programs, and certainly a scarcity of funds for new expenditures. Dealing with this stress, rather than proposing new programs, has become the central issue in budgeting.[10]

For the presidency, fiscal stress has been a strange sort of empowering factor: the problem of restraining or cutting spending, or just ordering priorities in the budget, demands a comprehensive approach to budgeting. That demand strengthens the president's hand in executive policymaking.

The developments combine to give the contemporary political agenda a shape that is different than before. The new political agenda separates late twentieth century politics from the era of the modern presidency.

THE BUDGET AS THE CENTRAL INSTRUMENT FOR GOVERNING

One of the most significant developments in the American political environment has been the growing prominence of the budget in public affairs. Indeed, it is fair to say that the budget has become the central instrument for governing in the United States.

This situation represents a new age in American government. As long as the federal government has had a budget (since the 1920s), it has been an important engine of policymaking. But it is only in recent years that the budget has taken on this central role.

The annual cycle of budget making is now the most fundamentally important act of the government. It not only allocates national fiscal resources, but sets national priorities, influences the shape and direction of the economy, and conditions all other policy decisions made in the executive and legislative branches. Budgeting has become the focus and the battleground for most of the significant policy questions of the day, from the state of education to the future of defense and arms control.

How is it that the budget is so important? The answer lies in three factors that characterize budgeting in contemporary American government: 1) the use of the budget for several purposes; 2) the prominence of budgetary issues due to fiscal stress; and, 3) the nature of the budget process.

The Multipurpose Budget

The most basic purpose of the federal budget, or of any governmental budget, is to pay the cost of government operations. But the U. S. budget also serves several other functions: setting national priorities, managing the economy, and distributing income.[11]

In many ways, the budget is the most effective device for setting priorities, because the amount allocated for any program reflects (even unconsciously) how important that item is to the president and Congress.

Since the budget is a compromise between the executive and the legislature (even if an unsatisfactory one), it is a better portrait of national priorities than the president's agenda or party platforms. Whereas those latter lists of priorities are proposals, the budget is a fait accompli.

Most activities of modern government require money, so the budget sets priorities among the many competing goals of the nation. It specifies just how important are the Strategic Defense Initiative, the school lunch program, farm price supports, AMTRAK, enforcement of environmental protection laws, the Smithsonian Institution, and a host of other activities, in the contest for national fiscal resources.

The budget also affects the management of the economy. The overall shape of the budget, and any attendant deficit or surplus, affects interest rates, inflation, and general economic growth. Ever since the Keynesian revolution of the 1930s, when the budget became an overt instrument of economic policy, federal spending has been a key factor in directing the national economy. Even specific spending programs, such as farm price supports, research funding (for defense or to fight AIDS), and loan guarantees (for students, Chrysler, or homeowners), are tools of economic policy.[12]

Finally, the budget is the most important governmental device for distributing income. Through direct transfer payments to individuals (Social Security, AFDC, etc.), subsidies, federal construction projects, and other payments, the national government distributes and redistributes wealth.[13]

The cumulative effect of these functions is to place the budget at the center of the U. S. government. Even in the age of regulation, the budget acts as one of the most important determinants of actual government policy. Regulation depends on the monitoring and enforcement of rules applied to businesses and individuals (as in stopping illegal waste disposal or policing insider stock trading), and those activities in turn depend on funding. Changes in funding for regulatory activities has a direct impact on the amount and character of government regulation. So, whether the United States is acting as the "positive state" or the "regulatory state," contemporary governance is driven by the multipurpose budget.

The Prominence of Budgetary Issues

For most of American history since World War II, the budget and budget deficits were regarded much as Mark Twain said of the weather:

everyone talked about deficits, but no one really did anything about them. Deficits were a perennial issue, but also a relatively constant feature of national policy: both parties contributed to deficit spending, and from 1946 to 1981 the national debt (as measured in 1982 dollars) remained essentially level in real-dollar terms.[14] Budgetary issues were a fixture of American politics, but did not dominate the public debate.

In 1981 that situation changed. Deficits rose sharply, from about 5 percent to approximately 20 percent of the budget.[15] The gross federal debt, which had been steadily declining as a share of GNP since 1950, rose dramatically. By fiscal 1986, the deficit had risen to a record $220.7 billion, raising the total national debt from about 27 percent of GNP in 1981 to about 42 percent.[16]

During the years of the Reagan Administration, the deficit became the most prominent issue in American politics. The president and his critics exchanged accusations about responsibility for huge deficits, and the question of what to do about them became central to political debate. The new budgetary politics was different from the old in that 1) deficits were now regarded as a problem that demanded action, and 2) deficits were now seen as a constraint on spending. As a result, ideas that had once been dismissed as unworkable—such as a line-item veto for the president,[17] a constitutional amendment requiring a balanced budget,[18] and automatic deficit reduction measures[19]—were given considerable attention.

A turning point came with the passage of the Balanced Budget Act of 1985.[20] That law represented the new prominence of budgetary issues. It proposed to solve the deficit crisis of the 1980s, and in its failure to do so, framed the politics of deficits for the future. The law established ambitious deficit reduction targets for budgets through 1991, at which time the budget was to be balanced. An important and controversial feature of the act was the sequestration process, whereby spending would be automatically cut if appropriations voted by Congress exceeded that year's target deficit level by $10 billion.[21]

The law was challenged as unconstitutional, and in 1986 the Supreme Court ultimately struck down important aspects of the automatic cutting process.[22] Soon, the annual deficit targets fell by the wayside,[23] with only the general goal of lower deficits remaining.

The result of the rise and fall of the balanced budget law was that the deficit became an environmental factor conditioning policymaking for the foreseeable future. Many economic forecasts predicted that deficits could shrink due to economic growth, but only if federal spending did not rise faster than inflation and no serious economic slump occurred.[24] In short, "living with deficits" was what national policymakers would have to do.[25]

This situation is otherwise known as fiscal stress. It means that budgetary issues will be a prominent feature of national politics for a long time. Even if the deficit is reduced to levels considered "normal" in the 1970s, national policymakers will be constrained by the need to avoid the "deficit out of control" atmosphere of the early 1980s. If deficits cannot be reduced to earlier levels, the pressure will be even greater. Either way, fiscal stress will condition policymaking for the rest of the century.

That situation will bolster the power of the president within the executive branch and induce future presidents to maintain "top-down" budgeting. The government-wide perspective and control that Ronald Reagan needed to advance his ambitious fiscal agenda will also be needed by his successors, whatever their goals. So, the prominence of budgetary issues in contemporary politics will reinforce the budgetary prerogatives of the post-modern presidency.

The Nature of the Budget Process

The process of budget making supplies further evidence of how the budget has become the central instrument for governing the United States. Through that aspect of budgeting called reconciliation, the process provides the means for the budget to influence the shape of a wide array of federal programs.[26]

Reconciliation is a device that enables Congress to alter existing statutes in order to bring them into line with appropriations in the annual budget. That means that the budget not only determines appropriation levels, but can be used to do just that, although not to the same degree every year.[27]

The significance of reconciliation is twofold. First, in concert with omnibus appropriations (i.e., packaging all appropriations together, rather than in several bills as was done before 1980), reconciliation gives the budget preeminence in setting national priorities, allocating resources, and shaping public programs. In short, it means that the budget acts as the engine and the rudder of federal policy.

Second, reconciliation offers what has been in recent years the only politically feasible means for controlling entitlement programs.[28] These programs, which include Social Security, AFDC, veterans' compensation, food stamps, Medicaid and Medicare, and other benefits, are different from discretionary spending. Indeed, "Authorizations for entitlements constitute a binding obligation on the part of the Federal Government, and eligible recipients have a legal recourse if the obligation is not fulfilled."[29]

Entitlements are often described as "uncontrollable" spending (along with interest payments on the national debt), although that comment is more politically than legally accurate. These programs are uncontrollable as long as their provisions (e.g., eligibility rules, automatic indexing of benefits for inflation) are unchanged: the funds necessary to support each program are determined by who is eligible and for what they are eligible. Changing the rules is politically difficult for several reasons; not the least of these is the fact that many entitlement programs are supported by large, vocal, and well-organized clientele groups.[30]

Entitlements exact distributed costs and deliver concentrated benefits, so for many years it was politically difficult to limit them and easier for Congress and presidents to let them continue apace. Consequently, entitlements grew continuously from the middle of the 1960s through the 1970s. By 1974, they constituted over 40 percent of federal spending, and would continue expanding for another decade. The term "uncontrollable" was applied more and more frequently.

That trend began to change in 1980, when the reconciliation process was first used to package many changes together (thus diminishing the responsibility of individual legislators for specific program changes) and to make them binding.[31] In 1981, the first Reagan budget would go even further. From that time, reconciliation was the key to controlling entitlements. In the years 1981–1985, reconciliation reduced entitlement outlays by as much as 39 percent for guaranteed student loans, 28 percent for child nutrition, 13.8 percent for food stamps, and 90 percent for trade adjustment assistance.[32]

The result of these changes, whatever their relative merits as public policy, was that reconciliation provided a way to control the "uncontrollable." Combined with its significance for reshaping existing laws and programs in the annual budget cycle, reconciliation advanced the trend of centralizing governance in the budget. Many of the most significant public decisions of the nation, once made through the law-writing process, are now made in the budgetary process.

The implications for the presidency are clear. Even if future presidents have expansive goals, they will have to promote their ends through the budget process. That is the new battlefield on which the major battles between the president and Congress are fought. Because of the centrality of the budget to governing, future presidents will jealously guard the budgetary prerogatives of the post-modern presidency.

THE NEW ELECTORAL POLITICS

As the nation's highest office, the presidency occupies a special place in American electoral politics. It is part of the party system, but distinct from congressional or state and local parties. The presidential nomination and campaign contest is the centerpiece of national politics, but it is a highly individualized process. To a great extent, presidential electoral politics exists in a world of its own.

That world has changed in the last two decades. The electoral system and the electorate are not the same as they were for much of postwar American history. These changes appear most clearly in three areas: changes in the party system; the rise of the entrepreneurial nominating system; and, the changing electorate. The result is a new electoral politics that distinguishes post-modern presidential selection from the past.

Changes in the Party System

Political parties in the United States have always been unique by world standards. They are less hierarchical, less disciplined, and less ideological than in other democratic nations. Moreover, they reflect and extend, rather than counteract, the American system of separation of powers and federalism. So, party politics in the United States has several centers of gravity.[33]

In recent years, the centers of gravity have shifted. At the presidential nominating level, influence has moved from state and local party "bosses" to party activists.[34] The growth of primaries and rule changes opening up the nominating process are responsible for this change. In congressional and many state elections, national party institutions have gained considerable importance in candidate recruitment and campaign support, roles they never had before.[35] The parties, thought to be dead or dying only a decade ago, have been revived and changed.

The changes of the past twenty years have made the party system much more participatory than before, so party activists and primary voters have tremendous influence over presidential nominations.[36] They have also opened the nomination process to public scrutiny, so giving the media a greater role.[37] The result of these changes is that the nomination process is a fluid and individualized one. Indeed, it is entrepreneurial in character.

The Entrepreneurial Nominating Process

The most fundamental characteristic of presidential selection in the new electoral politics is its entrepreneurial nature. Prospective presidential candidates self-select themselves to run for office, build their own campaign organizations, strategies, and circles of advisors, raise money for themselves, and seek nomination and then election on their own. By ''selling'' themselves to the voters, the media, and their parties, these entrepreneur-candidates reach the White House.

The structure of this entrepreneurial system has few fixed rules. In each presidential election since 1968, the parties (particularly the Democrats) have altered their rules.[38] Moreover, the timing and choice of nominating devices (primary, caucus, type of primary, etc.) are made on the state level, and subject to frequent change.[39] The chief rules for candidates are to start early, be prepared, and be flexible.

In this entrepreneurial process, ''outsiders'' have as much a chance of winning nomination and election as ''insiders.'' That is because the reformed nominating system allows anyone who has the ability to win votes to seek the nomination. Moreover, the long and self-managed campaign system benefits candidates with experience and time to run. For a long period in modern American history, the U.S. Senate was regarded as the chief vantage point for launching a presidential campaign. In the new system, ''outsider'' candidates (usually governors) are perhaps even more important: two ex-governors in a row (Carter and Reagan) won the office, in 1976 and 1980, and the 1988 field of candidates includes several contenders with primarily state-level gubernational experience (Chuck Robb, Pierre du Pont, Michael Dukakis). These officials are free of the taxing obligations faced by incumbent members of Congress. Senators seeking the presidency now often feel the need to leave the Senate, as did Gary Hart and Howard Baker, in order to have enough time both to run and to manage their own campaigns.[40]

The victor in this contest is a political entrepreneur who is able to survive and triumph in such an environment. It is no surprise, then, that post-modern presidents tend to govern through public politics, to employ a "general secretariat" for managing government, and to think in terms of their presidential prerogatives. The first of these employs a skill that won the candidate a victory. The second parallels the candidate's personal organization for winning the nomination and election. And the last of these is a perquisite that sets officeholders apart from candidates: presidents have powers they can rely upon, candidates have only persuasion and appeals. Post-modern presidents are engaged in a permanent campaign, waged largely on television for voter support,[41] so they use prerogative powers to enhance their chances of success.

The Changing Electorate

Just as the system has changed, so has the electorate changed. The number of voters in the 25–44 age group has increased sharply, old racial, ethnic, and occupational clusters have been disintegrating, and the economy is moving rapidly toward an information and service orientation, away from manufacturing.[42]

The results of these demographic changes, as well as greater mobility in the population and the rise of a new political agenda, is that old coalitions and voter alignments have broken down. The New Deal/Great Society coalition is certainly gone, and political observers are now locked in a debate about a possible partisan realignment.[43]

While that debate is far from over, this much can be said with certainty: the old electoral alignments are gone. The once-said Democratic South now also votes Republican; political power has been shifting south and west for many years, leaving behind the old industrial East and Midwest; and voters now identify with the Republican Party in about the same proportions as with the Democratic Party.[44] These trends indicate that something is afoot, although it is not clear just what.

In addition, there has been an explosion of interest groups involved in national politics. Where once only a few organized interests were significant—labor, business, certain ethnic groups—today, American politics is characterized by an incredible jumble of interests. These groups—ideological, economic, religious, social, ethnic, racial, and otherwise—have made politics much more fragmented than it used to be.

What do these changes mean for the presidency? They mean that the voters, as Everett Carl Ladd has put it, are "up for grabs."[45] They are sensitive to the pull of leaders and issues. In short, the electorate is in flux, and successful presidential candidates will be those who attract a following in such an environment.

Candidates with that kind of appeal will likely stand apart from the rest of their party, because they will be drawing on personal qualities, use of the media, and the issues of current interest at the time. They will then become post-modern presidents, because the modern presidency of their predecessors makes little sense in this new political environment.

THE MEDIA AGE

A fourth characteristic of the contemporary political environment is the importance of the news media to campaigning and governing in the United States. Through the media, particularly television, politics in the United States has been transformed into an intensely-reported spectator sport.

Although it existed in the 1940s, television acquired an important role in national politics only in the 1960s and 1970s. It is now the dominant medium of political communication in the United States: presidents can "go public" only because of television; congressional hearings and proceedings are now televised; televised political debates and press conferences have a special niche in political life; and, use of television advertisements now constitutes probably the most important aspect of any candidate's campaign tactics.[46]

The coming of this media age has brought a number of changes to American government. It has opened government at all levels, but particularly in Washington, to greater scrutiny. It has made national politics much more personalized, because politicians reach out to voters directly, past their parties, institutions, and other intermediaries. It has emphasized image and appearance in politics, but appearance has not overridden substance so much as it has affected the way that substantive matters are presented. In short, the media has brought the political fray into individual homes, and in doing so moved the political battleground from the stump and the legislative chamber to the airwaves.[47]

Much can and has been said about the effect of the news media on the conduct of the presidency, and Chapter 6 will examine these issues in more depth. But the media age is a fundamental characteristic of the larger political environment as well, and it affects Congress and other aspects of American politics beyond the presidency. As such, the media age encourages public politics throughout the political system, not just in the presidency.[48] Moreover, by personalizing politics, it reinforces other recent developments, including the entrepreneurial nominating process (which could only work effectively with television) and the consolidation of administrative and budgetary prerogatives in the presidency (because it is the president, rather than the bureaucrats "off-camera," who must take responsibility for the Executive Branch before the voters).

THE NEW CONGRESS

In the aftermath of Watergate and the upheavals of the 1960s, Congress began changing after the 1974 election. That election brought to Capitol Hill a bevy of new members impatient for change. They were not prepared to bide their time serving "apprenticeships" while the "inner club" in each house of Congress ran things, hoping one day to gain some power by virtue of seniority. Instead they wanted to change things, to shake up the "clubby" old Congress, and they did just that.[49]

The result of congressional reforms in the 1970s was the eventual creation of a "new" Congress, one distinctly different from its predecessor. This new Congress was a much more open and individualized institution than it had ever been, and the conduct of congressional business would never be the same.[50]

Much has been written on the new Congress, and it is not the point of this discussion to repeat the work of others.[51] Rather what is relevant here are the effects of congressional change on the president's political environment. In that regard, two general aspects of the new Congress are significant: 1) the open Congress; and, 2) the individualized Congress.

The Open Congress

The new Congress is a rather open legislative assembly. Its deliberations, conduct of business, and structure of power are quite removed from the days when Sam Rayburn's informal "Board of Education" gathered a few powerful members together to chart a course for the "clubby" Congress.[52] Today, cameras record all but the most sensitive aspects of congressional operations, from committee meetings to floor proceedings. Today, power is dispersed to committees, their subcommittees, individual members with substantive expertise (often quite junior), and clusters of members who share similar interests or opinions. Today, the heirs of the once-powerful committee "barons" (i.e., chairmen) of yesterday are coordinators who have influence but little power of command.

In the open congressional environment, there are no clear centers of power. There is power, but it is widely dispersed and held more tenuously than before. Nor is there much secrecy, except on a limited number of national security issues. Legislators' comments and votes are recorded, broadcast, and available for public inspection.[53] Consequently, votes are won by assembling coalitions for that vote alone, with individual members concerned about how that vote will be received back home.

The open Congress makes insider bargaining more difficult, because neither congressional leaders nor presidents can count on powerful chairmen or other influential members to deliver votes. But it also makes public politics easier, because a member's position on an issue, whether in committee or on the floor, is a matter of public record. Individual members are thus more vulnerable to constituent pressures, but pressure must be applied in more places. Conversely, members in tune with their constituents can resist a considerable amount of partisan or presidential pressure.

The Individualized Congress

Just as it is open, the new Congress is a highly individualized assembly. Individual members can and do develop influence, usually through substantive expertise, without serving a period of apprenticeship.

This individualization means that members who lack seniority or a base of committee support can still shape policy. Senator Phil Gramm, in his first term in the upper house, was the co-author and architect of the Balanced Budget Act of 1985. Four relatively junior members of Congress—Bill Bradley, Jack Kemp, Robert Kasten, and Richard Gephardt—contributed substantively to the overhaul of the tax code in 1986.

Members can be influential because staff resources are available to subcommittees and individuals. Each member of Congress heads what one Senator termed a "mini-conglomerate" of attorneys, Ph.D.s, clerical personnel, casework managers, media-relations staff, and other aides.[54] Staff resources give each Senator or Congressman the ability to play a somewhat independent role in the legislative process: introducing legislation, exploring new ideas, constructing compromises, assuming a visible position on a current issue, tracking legislation, and keeping up with several competing demands on the member's time and attention.[55]

At the same time, the same television camera that opened Congress has facilitated its individualization. The use of television and all other forms of mass media give members a platform from which to reach their own constituents from Washington, a larger audience, and other policymakers. As Norman Ornstein has explained, there are strong incentives for members of Congress to "go public":

This trend toward personal publicity provided, in contrast to the Rayburn era, a range of tangible and possible outside incentives. No longer did a member have to play by inside rules to receive inside rewards or avoid inside setbacks. One could "go public" and be rewarded by national attention; national attention in turn could provide ego gratification, social success in Washington, the opportunity to run for higher political office, or, by highlighting an issue, policy success.[56]

Another device that promotes individualization is the caucus. There are now a wide array of caucuses in Congress, some with formal structure, offices, and staffs, that allow clusters of like-minded members to assemble in support of common interests. There are almost one hundred of these organizations, ranging from the Democratic Study Group (225 members) to the Friends of Ireland (80 members), the Senate Wine Caucus (10 members), and the Congressional Task Force on Afghanistan (19 members). Caucuses allow members to promote their interests and goals outside of the traditional party structure, as well as to develop expertise and form the nucleus for legislative coalitions. Membership in caucuses allows Senators and Congressmen to act outside of the committee structure and to do so as individuals.

The result of this individualization is that Congress operates through a decentralized process built on shifting coalitions of members. There are what Samuel Kernell calls "protocoalitions" for a variety of issues: often existing in the caucuses, but not pre-formed reliable party coalitions, ideological or interest-based alliances, or leadership-inspired groupings of members.[57] Consequently, a coalition must be built for each major vote, whether by activist members, leaders, or the president. The open, individualized Congress is unwieldy.

But it is also more actively involved in policy formulation than its predecessor. Because the legislature is open to members' interests and initiatives, and staff resources so widely available, Congress is capable of playing a larger role in constructing policy than it was in the era of the modern presidency. Congress does not speak with one voice, but the many voices issuing forth are louder than in the days of FDR and Lyndon Johnson.

To that extent, the American political system has become more Madisonian in character. Where the era of the traditional presidency saw Congress as the chief architect of national policy, and the modern presidency as the guide for legislation, the post-modern political era features two strong political branches competing to direct the course of national affairs.[58]

POLICYMAKING BY ADMINISTRATIVE AND JUDICIAL BODIES

The final aspect of the new political environment that is relevant to the presidency is the fact that many significant national policy decisions are now made by administrative and judicial bodies. Policymaking power does not reside only in the elected branches of government, but now exists in these unelected units. In the era of the post-modern presidency, the political system has become less focused on direct presidential policymaking and refocused on the president's ability to shape or influence a variety of policymaking institutions.

The bureaucracy and the judiciary have emerged in recent decades as important policymaking bodies. Many of the most far-reaching decisions affecting national life were made by these unelected bodies, from rules governing school integration and abortion rights to regulations on consumer product safety and insider stock trading.[59]

Moreover, this situation is unlikely to change dramatically in the near future. For all the criticism of court-ordered busing and expansion of abortion rights, the power of the courts to make policy has not been seriously challenged by the president and Congress. Although President Reagan and his Attorney General attacked judicial activism, there is no indication that the Supreme Court would quit making policy decisions.[60] At the same time, despite the deregulation efforts of recent years, curbing many excesses of regulatory power, the broad fundamental power of independent regulatory commissions is not in jeopardy. There is little sentiment in Congress or the public to repeal the basic structure of regulation.

So, there is now significant power in unelected bodies to make public decisions. This situation marks a change from the heyday of the modern presidency, when executive leadership of Congress was the primary means of shaping and reshaping national policy.

This change is the source of the "surrogate presidency." A postmodern president makes his mark on his time and the national future as much through his judicial and regulatory appointments as through his legislative or foreign policy initiatives. Whether the president is able to make many of these appointments or only a few, and regardless of whether or not they perform as he hopes, a president's appointees will make authoritative decisions that will be as much part of the president's legacy as his legislative record.

THE PRESIDENCY IN THE NEW ENVIRONMENT

The post-modern presidency is intimately connected to this new political environment. That environment shapes the selection of the Chief Executive, affects the issues he confronts and the means by which he confronts them, and the structure of the government in which he acts.

How do post-modern presidents govern in this environment? The answer is that they do not. The post-modern presidency does not govern, but is the premier part of a governing system. For all the characterization of the American system as presidential government, it is no such creature. Rather, it is a creature with several heads. How presidents work within that system is the real issue: what prerogatives the president possesses, and how he uses them; how well he manages to keep his own house in order; how he relates to his governmental and public audiences; and, how he operates in the politics of the late twentieth century.

The metamorphosis that has occurred in the presidency and its political environment over the past two decades demonstrates how much American politics have changed since the days of FDR and LBJ. The remainder of this book will be a closer look at the features and operations of the post-modern presidency.

NOTES

1. Quoted in Donald Lambro, "What did the 1986 election tell us?" *The World & I* (January 1987): 106; and, Jones, "Keeping faith," p. 441.

2. Seidman, op. cit. See also Samuel Beer, "In search of a new public philosophy," in *The New American Political System*, pp. 33–44; and, Jones, "Keeping faith," pp. 441–2.

3. See Lawrence D. Brown, *New Policies, New Politics: Government's Response to Government's Growth* (Washington: Brookings Institution, 1983); Roger Noll, *Reforming Regulation* (Washington: Brookings Institution, 1971); James Q. Wilson, *The Politics of Regulation* (New York: Basic Books, 1980); and Otis L. Graham, Jr., *Toward a Planned Society* (New York: Oxford University Press, 1976).

4. Ball, op. cit.

5. Hugh Heclo and Rudolph G. Penner, "Fiscal and political strategy in the Reagan Administration," in *The Reagan Presidency*, pp. 21–47.

6. Ibid.

7. Paul E. Peterson, "The new politics of deficits," in *The New Direction in American Politics*, p. 397.

8. *National Journal*, November 1, 1986, p. 2628. Of course, deficits had been around for years, but during the Reagan Administration came to loom much larger in the economy.

9. Ibid.

10. See ibid., pp. 2627–30 for a survey of how coping with deficits has become the central concern of budget planners and policymakers.

11. Heclo, "Executive budget making," p. 265.

12. For a good discussion of the government's role in economic affairs, see Michael Reagan, *The Managed Economy* (New York: Oxford University Press, 1963). See also Herbert Stein, *The Fiscal Revolution in America* (Chicago: University of Chicago Press, 1969).

13. For a brief but useful survey of income distribution and redistribution policies, see Randall Ripley and Grace Franklin, *Policy Implementation and Bureaucracy*, 2nd ed. (Chicago: Dorsey Press, 1986), pp. 71–77.

14. Peterson, p. 367.

15. Ibid., p. 367.

16. *National Journal*, November 1, 1986, p. 2628.

17. For a survey of this issue, see Thomas E. Cronin and Jeffrey J. Weill, "An item veto for the President?" *Congress and the Presidency* 12 (Autumn 1985): 127–152. In 1985, the Senate nearly passed an item veto proposal, with several notable liberals (especially Senator Kennedy) voting for the bill; see *National Journal*, August 3, 1985, p. 1807.

18. The balanced-budget amendment never went too far in Congress, but influenced action on the Balanced Budget Act of 1985 (Gramm-Rudman-Hollings). See *National Journal*, October 19, 1985, p. 2395, and November 16, 1985, pp. 2586–8.

19. P. L. 99–177. For a concise explanation of the law, see U. S. Congress, Senate, Committee on the Budget, *Gramm-Rudman-Hollings and the Congressional Budget Process*, Committee Print, 99th Cong., 1st sess., December 1985.

20. Ibid.

21. Ibid.

22. *National Journal*, July 11, 1986, p. 1721.

23. *National Journal*, November 1, 1986, p. 2627.

24. Ibid., pp. 2628–30.

25. Ibid., p. 2627.

26. McMurty, p. 39. See also Allan Schick, *Reconciliation and the Congressional Budget Process* (Washington: American Enterprise Institute, 1981).

27. Ibid., pp. 38–45 and 49–54. See also Gregory B. Mills and John L. Palmer, eds., *Federal Budget Policy in the 1980s* (Washington: Urban Institute Press, 1984).

28. A similar observation is made in R. Kent Weaver, "Controlling entitlements," in *The New Direction in American Politics*, edited by John E. Chubb and Paul E. Peterson (Washington: Brookings Institution, 1985), p. 333.

29. U. S. General Accounting Office, *A Glossary of Terms Used in the Federal Budget Process*, 3rd. ed., PAD–81–27 (Washington: GAO, 1981), p. 57.

30. Weaver, pp. 310–311. See also *Congressional Quarterly Weekly Report*, November 1, 1986, pp. 2790–7.

31. Ibid., p. 333. See also McMurty, p. 38–39.

32. Ibid., p. 325.

33. The best introduction to American political parties is Frank J. Sorauf, *Party Politics in America*, 5th ed. (Boston: Little, Brown, 1984). For a discussion of changes in the party system, see Kayden and Mahe, op. cit.

34. Crotty and Jackson, p. 51.

35. Kayden and Mahe, p. 4.

36. Crotty and Jackson, loc. cit.

37. Ibid., pp. 74–8.

38. Ibid., p. 32.

39. For the latest array of rules and scheduling of primaries and caucuses,

see New York *Times*, November 10, 1986, pp. 1 and 8. See also William Safire, "The '88 campaign begins," New York *Times*, October 13, 1986, p. 19.

40. For a discussion of the new advantage to "outsiders," see Samuel Kernell, "Campaigning, governing, and the contemporary Presidency," in *The New Direction in American Politics*, pp. 117–41.

41. See Kernell, p. 138.

42. New York *Times*, September 5, 1986, p. 1.

43. That debate is a complex one. For a sampling of the arguments and evidence, see Nelson W. Polsby, "The Democratic nomination and the evolution of the party system," in *The American Elections of 1984*, pp. 36–65, edited by Austin Ranney, an American Enterprise Institute Book (Durham, NC: Duke University Press, 1985); James Q. Wilson, "Realignment at the top, dealignment at the bottom," in *The American Elections of 1984*, pp. 297–311; John E. Chubb and Paul E. Peterson, "Realignment and institutionalization," in *The New Direction in American Politics*, pp. 1–32; and Everett Carl Ladd, "Alignment and realignment: Where are the voters going?" *The Ladd Report*, #3 (New York: W. W. Norton, 1986).

44. Ibid., p. 2.

45. Ibid., p. 27.

46. On the intense use of television in the 1986 congressional campaigns, see *National Journal*, November 1, 1986, pp. 2619–26.

47. On the role of the media in American politics, see Doris A. Graber, *Mass Media and American Politics* (Washington: Congressional Quarterly Press, 1980). On its importance throughout the 1984 presidential campaign, see Michael J. Robinson, "Where's the beef? Media and media elites in 1984," in *The American Elections of 1984*, pp. 166–202.

48. Kernell, *Going Public*, Ch. 1.

49. For a clever contrast between the old and the new Congresses, see Norman Ornstein, "The open Congress meets the President," in *Both Ends of the Avenue*, pp. 185–94.

50. Ibid., pp. 193–194.

51. See Thomas Mann and Norman J. Ornstein, eds., *The New Congress*; Anthony King, ed., *Both Ends of the Avenue*; Rieselbach, *Congressional Reform*; Kernell, pp. 29–35; and Steven S. Smith, "New patterns of decision-making in Congress," in *The New Direction in American Politics*, pp. 203–34.

52. See Robert A. Caro, *The Years of Lyndon Johnson, Volume I: The Path to Power* (New York: Vintage Books, 1981), pp. 452–453.

53. Ornstein, "The open Congress," pp. 195–200.

54. Senator J. Bennett Johnston, interview with author, July 26, 1977. See also Ryan J. Barilleaux, "Aide's-eye view of the Senate," *Christian Science Monitor*, May 15, 1978, p. 21.

55. For a more in-depth look at congressional staffs, see Malbin, op. cit.

56. Kernell, *Going Public*, pp. 26–32.

57. Ibid., Ch. 1.

58. This argument is in direct contrast to Lawrence Dodd's theory of the "cycles of power." Dodd assumes, from a misunderstanding of Madison, that Congress can only be assertive if it operates as a tightly-run machine. See Dodd, "Congress, the Constitution, and the crisis of legitimation," in *Congress Reconsidered*, 2d ed., edited by Lawrence C. Dodd and Bruce I. Oppenheimer (Washington: Congressional Quarterly Press, 1981), pp. 390–420.

59. See Chapter 1, section on "Vicarious Policymaking" and attendant notes.

60. The appointments of Chief Justice William Rehnquist and Associate Justice Scalia have not promised to end judicial policymaking power, although a Rehnquist Court alters the direction of judicial policymaking.

4   Post-Modern Prerogatives

The new political environment of the presidency has had an interesting effect on the conduct of that office. It has not only encouraged presidents to rely on their prerogatives to govern, but to expand the scope of those prerogatives as well. In responding to such incentives, and aided by developments in law, technology, and politics, presidents over the past two decades ushered in a new era of prerogative power. They also helped to shape the post-modern presidency.

Writing in the 1970s, Richard Pious emphasized the importance of prerogative power to presidents caught between public expectations and the frustrations of collaborative government.[1] He concluded, in a period when presidential power was at a low point, that "prerogatives are still seen by the White House as the antidote to paralysis."[2] Prerogative power allows the president to break through the apparent logjam of "separate institutions sharing power" that inhibits governmental action, of whatever sort, in order to influence events.

Thus it is not surprising that the revival of prerogative power has been a fundamental feature of the post-modern presidency. Moreover, some of the most significant presidential prerogatives are new ones. These post-modern prerogatives are congruent with an age in which so much of governing occurs through budget making and administrative action, rather than legislation.

The consequence of these post-modern prerogatives is that the presidency now possesses a wider array of powers for influencing the direction of national policy than it did in earlier periods. Future presidents, whatever their policy goals, will want these prerogatives in order to act and to deliver on the promises they have made.

A MORE COMPLETE PRESIDENCY

Since the 1960s, the conventional wisdom among students of the presidency has been that presidential power is dramatically uneven. As Aaron Wildavsky, the author of this view, has put it:

The United States has one President, but it has two presidencies; one presidency is for domestic affairs, and the other is concerned with defense and foreign policy. Since World War II, Presidents have had much greater success in controlling the nation's defense and foreign policies than in dominating its domestic policies.[3]

Wildavsky's "two presidencies" thesis has been the subject of some controversy, but is generally accepted as an accurate portrayal of presidential power.

Yet that thesis fits the modern presidency much better than the post-modern office. As prerogative power has been revived in the past two decades, a more complete presidency has emerged: presidential prerogatives in budgetary policymaking and administrative clearance now exist to complement the president's traditional powers in foreign affairs.

Do these changes mean that there are no longer two presidencies? No, but Wildavsky's dichotomy of presidential power is less appropriate than it was once. Presidents still have a harder time getting their way in domestic policy, but their resources in that area are greater than they were when Wildavsky coined the phrase "the two presidencies." By consolidating control over the executive budget process and the making of administrative regulations, the post-modern president is now able to deal with Congress from a position of greater strength than his modern predecessors.

Of course, the president also faces a legislature more willing and more able to oppose the president. So, post-modern presidents apply pressure on Congress by manipulating their prerogatives and resorting to public politics. The more complete presidency cannot govern by prerogative alone, but now possesses weapons its forerunners lacked.

THE PREROGATIVE OF ADMINISTRATIVE CLEARANCE

The development of the administrative clearance prerogative has given post-modern presidents a device for controlling, or at least influencing, the de facto legislative power possessed by federal executive agencies.

As federal government activities expanded in the twentieth century, Congress came increasingly to rely on administrative agencies for assistance in defining national policy. As Congress grew busier legislating in wider range of policy areas, it tended to delegate broad authority for specifying policy details to the administrative units that would implement the programs and laws it had enacted.[4] Rulemaking by executive agencies thus expanded dramatically, as these units took their widened power as a mandate to legislate.

Presidents tended to view this expansion of administrative power with alarm. First, granting rulemaking authority directly to administrative units bypassed the president, so the Chief Executive had little or no role in such activities.[5] That fact, combined with the growing size of the bureaucracy, led presidents to share the popular view that the federal bureaucracy was out of control.[6] Second, with increasing criticism of the costs that regulation imposed on businesses, presidents also tended to regard expanded regulatory power as bad policy.[7] So, from Richard Nixon forward, presidents attempted to rein in the rulemaking power and independence of the bureaucracy.

Nixon first asserted presidential power to oversee administrative rulemaking in 1971, with the establishment of the Quality of Life review process. This process, which was controversial throughout its existence, employed OMB to supervise the development of environmental, health and safety, consumer protection, and other rules.[8] The ostensible purpose of Quality of Life reviews was to ensure that new regulations were reconciled with other administration goals and contributed to the nation's overall "quality of life," but OMB's oversight tended to focus on the Environmental Protection Agency (EPA).[9] These reviews continued until shortly after Jimmy Carter's inauguration in 1977.

Gerald Ford followed his predecessor's example by extending regulatory review beyond EPA to all executive agencies.[10] Moreover, he introduced the criterion of "inflationary impact" to the process. His Executive Order 11,821 (1975) required that agencies assess the effect on inflation of all proposed "major" rules prior to their publication, with OMB supervising the process.[11] Each proposed rule was accompanied by an inflationary impact statement that was reviewed by the President's Council on Wage and Price Stability (COWPS), but each agency was the ultimate arbiter of its own rules.[12] This requirement not only expanded the president's oversight prerogatives, but also tended to induce better economic analysis of the effects of regulations.[13]

Jimmy Carter made presidential review of agency rulemaking a bipartisan activity. His E.O. 12,044 (1977) established a broader and more elaborate procedure for review of proposed regulations.[14] Agencies were required to analyze the anticipated effects of proposed "significant" rules (undefined), and each agency had to prepare a semi-annual agenda of forthcoming rulemaking plans.[15] Unlike his predecessors, however, President Carter did not use OMB for supervision of the process. Rather, supervisory authority was vested in three bodies: COWPS, a Regulatory Council, and a Regulatory Analysis Review Group. The two latter groups were essentially interagency committees and neither exercised coordinating or enforcement authority over the rulemaking agencies. The ultimate locus of decision in the Carter process was the agency proposing the rule.

Ronald Reagan carried these precedents to their logical conclusion: he instituted mandatory review of all "major" rules, prescribed a system of cost/benefit analysis that each proposed rule had to survive in order to be published, and required each agency to establish a regulatory agenda that would detail all regulatory activity either "planned or underway."[16]

Through E.O. 12,291 (1981) and E.O. 12,498 (1985), President Reagan consolidated presidential oversight of administrative rulemaking. OMB was charged with enforcement power in the administrative clearance process created by these Orders, thus giving the president's "general secretariat" special authority over the Executive Branch.

In the Reagan Administration, attention has been focused on EPA regulations, but that fact does not mean that administrative clearance has such limited potential. Rather, it has the potential to be a powerful tool for influencing administrative policymaking throughout the Executive Branch.

A good example of this potential can be seen in the Immigration Reform Act of 1986. That law, which reshaped U.S. policy regarding entry into the United States, gave broad power to the U.S. Immigration and Naturalization Service (INS) to write specific rules governing amnesty for aliens residing illegally in the United States. With administrative clearance, OMB could effectively shape the rules written pursuant to that act, thus influencing immigration policy as implemented.

The potential power of administrative clearance lies in its utility for presidents and its strong (although not unshakable) grounding in the president's constitutional and legal authority over the Executive Branch. President Reagan's two Executive Orders are essentially grounded in the president's Article II responsibility to "take care that the Laws be faithfully executed,"[17] and the Constitution's creation of a single Chief Executive. The Constitution specifies that "The Executive Power shall be vested in a President...,"[18] which proponents of administrative clearance argue is a provision that empowers the president to take charge of the Executive Branch.[19]

Presidents from Nixon through Reagan have interpreted their constitutional powers and responsibilities to mean that the president has the authority to supervise and oversee administrative rulemaking, even if Congress delegated to specific agencies the power to write regulations. Despite criticisms of administrative clearance that range from charges of unconstitutionality to attacks on its putative anti-EPA tone, presidents are likely to want to keep and employ this prerogative in the future.

Administrative clearance is a device that can serve the interests of presidents with a variety of policy goals. Mr. Reagan's OMB has focused on EPA in its regulatory review, but other presidents might direct it at other agencies. A president interested in trimming the defense budget, for example, might subject the Department of Defense to this process, whereas President Reagan exempted the Pentagon. A pro-regulation president might use administrative clearance to ensure that agency rules are sufficiently stringent to suit his goals. Finally, regardless of the policy goals of the incumbent, administrative clearance provides the president with a powerful tool for obtaining information about Executive Branch activities and exercising some supervisory power over the bureaucracy. Any president will want to keep such a tool.

Critics of administrative clearance may dispute the president's authority to exercise such review, but that prerogative is a defensible one.[20] It does make at least prima facie constitutional sense. Considering its utility to presidents, and despite whatever its relative policy merits may be, administrative clearance is likely to be a permanent fixture in the prerogative arsenal of the post-modern presidency.

THE IMPORTANCE OF BUDGETARY PREROGATIVES

Because the budget now serves as the central instrument for governing, the consolidation of presidential budgetary prerogatives is an important development in the national policy process. For the post-modern presidency now possesses power long sought by modern presidents: the power to intervene in the close relationship between executive agencies and Congress that exists because of the legislature's control of the federal purse strings.

When Congress reformed its budgetary process in 1974, it did so largely to arm itself for battle with the president and the Executive Branch. The period 1966–1973 had been marked by what Allan Schick called the "Seven-Year Budget War," in which the executive and legislative branches struggled over national spending priorities, taxes, and limits on the size of the budget.[21] Even with its largely decentralized process for drawing up budget requests, the executive seemed to have an advantage over Congress: decentralization was not absolute, and a president working within its constraints could take on the legislature with some degree of effectiveness. Congress, on the other hand, had a fragmented budget process, marked by conflicts between the appropriations and tax committees, as well as divided authority over spending authorizations and actual appropriations.[22] The Budget Act of 1974 was to give Congress a coherent and functional budget-making process, coordinated in each house by a Budget Committee.

The reformed process did not live up to expectations at first, but instead seemed to merely bring better order to business as usual. Presidents continued to worry about the close relations between agencies and congressional committees, while budget reformers in Congress lamented that the fragmented system had not been overthrown.[23]

All that began to change, however, late in the presidency of Jimmy Carter. In 1980, two important developments occurred: 1) for the first time, budget negotiations between the White House and congressional leaders moved budget decision making toward centralization and away from the fragmented agency–committee budget network; and, 2) the reconciliation provisions of the 1974 budget act were employed to instruct congressional committees on statutory changes necessary to achieve budgetary spending targets.[24] These precedents were revolutionizing budget making even as critics were pronouncing the death of presidential power.

The Carter precedents would be build upon by the Reagan Administration, which turned reconciliation into an instrument for comprehensive policy change and solidified OMB control over executive budget making. President Reagan needed these changes if he was to have any hope of achieving the dramatic budget changes he sought, and the reformed congressional process ironically served his needs.

As noted above, the president needed a government-wide perspective on the budget in order for Mr. Reagan to advance his policy goals. In the Executive Branch, that perspective was provided by OMB, which by 1982 had developed the technological capacity to give the president a comprehensive view of budget formulation. OMB had developed a Central Budget Management System (CBMS), a sophisticated computer program that enables OMB to track different budget proposals (presidential, House, Senate, etc.) and all modifications thereof, compare differences among them, and amend numbers according to revised economic forecasts.[25] In Congress, the government-wide view was provided by the two budget committees, which now assumed a central role in the budget-making process.

The upshot of these developments was that "top-down" executive budgeting was born, with the 1974 congressional process aiding the consolidation of new presidential prerogatives. Through OMB, post-modern presidents are able to control agency budget requests in a way that their modern predecessors would envy. Future presidents, whatever their policy goals, will not want to lose such control.

"Top-down budgeting" is accompanied by other related prerogatives. First, because he controls the budget request process and the budget is now the central instrument for governing, post-modern presidents can use the annual budget cycle to initial policy changes. For example, Ronald Reagan's draft budget for fiscal 1988 included a proposal to dramatically restructure the Medicare program of federal healthcare assistance for the elderly, as well as plans to alter the schedule of veteran's benefits provided by the government.[26] Substantive presidential legislative initiatives are now packaged in the central budget document, giving OMB and the president greater control over policy initiatives.

A second related prerogative is an expanded spending deferral power for the president. While the president's ability to impound funds appropriated by Congress, a source of contention in the "Seven-Year Budget War," was essentially ended by the Impoundment Act of 1974, the president still possesses the ability to defer spending. The 1974 Budget Act gave either house of Congress the power to stop such deferrals, but the president's hand was strengthened by the 1983 *Chadha* ruling.[27] Because the *Chadha* decision undercuts Congress' power to control presidential actions through the use of the legislative veto, particularly a one-house legislative veto, the provision of the 1974 law governing deferrals is probably dead. Therefore, the president may defer spending with impunity. On long-term spending projects, such as public works and military procurement, such deferrals constitute a de facto form of impoundment or even line-item veto. This prerogative, gained serendipitously by the Chief Executive, gives post-modern presidents one more weapon to use in their struggle to control national policy.

The consequence of all these budgetary prerogatives is that contemporary presidents have significant powers for influencing the operations of the single most important instrument for governing. These powers do not guarantee a president the budgetary outcomes he desires, but they do make him a formidable contender in a struggle over the federal purse.

PUPD AND ARMS-CONTROL PREROGATIVES

Perhaps the least-known and most subtle of post-modern presidential prerogatives lies in the area of arms control. Through that device known as parallel unilateral policy declarations (PUPD), U.S. arms control policy has in effect become a presidential prerogative.

Arms control was long an area in foreign affairs that seemed to allow limited presidential discretion. Ever since President Eisenhower's early discussions of arms control initiatives with the Soviet Union, Congress expressed concern about a president "negotiating away" too much of national defense. In 1961, when the Arms Control and Disarmament Act created an arms control agency attached to the State Department, Section 33 of that law explicitly limited the president's power:

no action shall be taken under this or any other law that will obligate the United States to disarm or to reduce or to limit the Armed Forces or armaments of the United States except pursuant to the treaty-making power of the President or unless further authorized by further affirmative legislation by the Congress of the United States.[28]

Later amendments went even further, specifically prohibiting the president from negotiating a treaty or agreement that would undermine the right of U.S. citizens to keep and bear arms.

Despite these strictures, however, Presidents Carter and Reagan were able to seize effective control of arms control policy and circumvent congressional involvement. In 1977, Carter extended the expiring SALT I Interim Agreement through the parallel issuance by the United States and the Soviet Union of identical statements pledging continued adherence to the defunct treaty if the other party did likewise.[29] In 1980, realizing that his Salt II treaty would not pass the Senate, he asked that it not be considered by that body. But SALT II was implemented nevertheless, again by parallel unilateral policy declarations.[30] When Ronald Reagan assumed office in 1981, he affirmed Carter's PUPD, a move analogous to one president's affirmation of an executive agreement concluded by a predecessor.[31] Then in 1985, when SALT II was to expire (despite its unratified status), Congress requested a statement of the president's intentions. Mr. Reagan responded that he would "go the extra mile" and continue to observe the limits of the treaty.[32] The following year, however, the president decided that Soviet violations of arms control made U.S. compliance impractical, and withdrew his support for SALT II.

Throughout this decade of non-agreements, Congress was little more than a spectator to arms control policymaking by presidential fiat. A move in Congress in 1977 to prevent the original PUPD precedent on SALT I failed, and from that time the legislature accepted these executive non-agreements.[33] In 1983, members of Congress praised Mr. Reagan's decision to "go the extra mile," and reserved their criticism for his Strategic Defense Initiative. In 1986, after the president abandoned SALT II, congressional criticism of Mr. Reagan gave the impression that there had indeed been an agreement. Some members even tried to mandate a return to U.S. compliance with the treaty, but to no avail.

The situation had taken a bizarre twist: many in Congress were now trying to coerce the president to exercise his recently acquired power. Arms control policy had indeed become a presidential prerogative. The president's traditional constitutional power to initiate negotiations was now accompanied by an ability to dictate agreements, or rather non-agreements.

What had happened to the requirements of Section 33? They seemed impotent in the shadowy face of PUPD. Because this sort of non-agreement is not clearly an agreement as specified in the arms control law, the president is free to act. The PUPDs used to implement and extend the two SALT agreements were intended precisely to support and serve as proxies for negotiated treaties, but both presidents involved denied that any agreements existed. In the twilight world between international agreements and no agreements whatsoever, PUPD promotes presidential autonomy.

Nor does the 1974 Case Act help to clarify the status of PUPD and the extent of presidential prerogative. That law requires that all international agreements other than treaties be transmitted to Congress within sixty days of their conclusion, but it is not clear whether the act applies to PUPD. The Case Act leaves to the Secretary of State the power to decide "whether an arrangement constitutes an international agreement,"[34] and the 1981 regulations implementing the law leave the issue unsettled.

Under the rules promulgated by the State Department, an "undertaking" to extend a treaty or agreement is itself an international agreement subject to the terms of the law. An agreement to implement another agreement is one as well.[35] But the rules state that intention to be bound is an important characteristic of an international agreement,[36] and U.S. presidents have declared that they did not intend to be bound by PUPDs. Therefore, the Case Act does not clearly apply to these non-agreements.

The upshot of these ambiguities is that the presidency has acquired decisive control over arms control policy. Arms control initiatives have always been in the president's domain, but until 1977 Congress played a role in shaping U.S. policy through its treaty powers and Section 33. Indeed, the nonbinding Jackson Amendment to the SALT I Interim Agreement (calling for numerical equality in superpower arsenals and accelerated defense research) indicated Congress' former ability to influence policy in this area.[37] In the age of the post-modern presidency, however, control over this policy area is in practice a presidential prerogative.

Such a prerogative is no small thing, because of the centrality of arms control issues to superpower relations in the late twentieth century. As the 1986 Reykjavik summit between President Reagan and Premier Gorbachev, the Strategic Defense Initiative, strategic force modernization, and other developments have all made clear, superpower defense and arms issues will be central to U.S. foreign policy for the foreseeable future. To that extent, an effective prerogative over arms control policy gives the president the power to shape the future without serious challenge from Congress.

How might presidents employ this prerogative? By using it skillfully, in concert with the president's control over negotiations, they can determine whether and in what form there will be future arms agreements. From 1980 to 1986, U.S. adherence to, reservations about, modifications of, and ultimately abandonment of SALT II were all dictated by the president. Both supporters and critics of that treaty had to take arms control on Mr. Reagan's terms, whether or not they liked those terms. A future under PUPD is a future of arms policy by executive fiat.

Of course the president will have to be careful about how he exercises this prerogative, but Congress is not likely to challenge his use of it. Even in the midst of the Iran-Contra scandal, with his credibility sagging, President Reagan was able to ignore congressional pressure to revive SALT II and instead ordered deployment of a B–52 bomber that exceeded the limitations of that treaty. Future presidents, whatever their goals in this area, will draw upon the precedents of the Carter–Reagan PUPD decade to dominate U.S. arms control policy. Strategic arms policy without significant congressional input is a distinct possibility.

IMPLICATIONS FOR FUTURE PRESIDENTS

The preceding discussion is not intended to suggest that the president can command public policy as he chooses, but to illuminate the expansion of presidential prerogatives that has occurred over the past few years. Even if the president needs public support to govern most effectively, which is why post-modern presidents tend to go public, and still must persuade Congress and the bureaucracy to go along with presidential plans, the prerogatives of the Chief Executive constitute a significant aspect of his power.

Prerogative power is back, and it exists even in the face of scandals, crises of confidence, and other limitations on the "power to persuade."

Because the president can influence and perhaps even shape administrative rulemaking, he can affect the implementation of policy. Because
of top-down budgeting and other fiscal powers, the president can use
the central instrument for governing to put his stamp on national life.
Because he can effectively shape arms control policy, the president can
influence the future course of world events. These prerogatives are post-
modern ones: they arise from and are suited for an age in which governing means regulating, budgeting, and summitry, rather than legislating and administering.

Future presidents will use and rely on the prerogatives gained in the
past two decades, because these powers enable the Chief Executive to
operate in the new political environment. The political system has become more Madisonian in character, because it now features two strong
branches competing to direct national policy. To operate in that system,
the presidency has become more Hamiltonian in nature: the post-modern
presidency combines aggressive exercises of presidential prerogatives
with vigorous public politics, in order to compete with an assertive
legislature whose members are themselves skillful at public relations.[38]

These post-modern prerogatives developed largely in a time of government retrenchment, yet their potential as presidential tools is not
limited to incumbents with the same goals as Ronald Reagan. Because
these prerogatives most significantly involve aiding the president's quest
to be master in his own house, they can and will serve presidents of
every political stripe.

A Note on *INS v. Chadha*

The 1983 Court ruling in the case of *INS v. Chadha* has been mentioned at several points in this book as an instance of the broadening
of the president's autonomy. While it is beyond the scope of this work
to consider the *Chadha* decision in depth, a few points ought to be
made about that ruling's effect on the post-modern presidency.

INS v. Chadha seriously wounded one of Congress' most effective
tools for restraining executive power: the legislative veto. According
to a brief prepared for the U.S. Senate, at least fifty-six statutes were
affected by the decision, including the War Powers Resolution, the
Congressional Budget and Impoundment Act of 1974, and several laws
delegating rulemaking power to executive officers.[39]

The *Chadha* decision did not exactly kill the legislative veto, however. As Daniel Franklin has made clear, Congress has several alternatives for either modifying the legislative veto to meet the Court's objections or using similar but different devices to restrain executive autonomy.[40] For example, Congress could expand the use of provisions that require executive agencies to "report and wait" on proposed actions. Or Congress could shorten the long leash it has given to many agencies for rulemaking. These and other moves would limit executive autonomy even more than the legislative veto did. The overriding point of Professor Franklin's analysis is that Congress can still limit the executive if it chooses to do so.

But the ease and convenience of the old legislative veto, especially where one house or even a committee could halt an executive decision, is gone. Congress will have to work all the harder to check the executive along these lines. To that extent, the president's skill at exercising his prerogatives will be crucial to the fate of the legislative veto: if presidents do not flagrantly invite congressional second-guessing, they could carry on indefinitely without Congress' resorting to Professor Franklin's alternatives; if they act in a fashion that stimulates a harsh congressional response, future presidents may wish for a return to the flexibility of the legislative veto.

No matter what the ultimate outcome, it is still too early to gauge the precise effects of the *Chadha* decision. At this point, however, it is safe to conclude that the ruling serves to expand executive autonomy. The remaining question is just how great that expansion will be.

CONCLUSION

Presidential power is more than the power to persuade. It is also the power to coerce. With the revival of prerogative power, the president has acquired important new tools with which to influence government. These tools will serve many goals and many presidents. By skillfully combining persuasion and coercion, post-modern presidents can advance their goals.

NOTES

1. Pious, p. 422.
2. Ibid., p. 422.

3. Aaron Wildavsky, "The two Presidencies," in *The Presidency*, edited by Aaron Wildavsky (Boston: Little, Brown, 1969), p. 230.

4. Rosenberg, pp. 185–95.

5. Ibid., p. 198.

6. Ibid., p. 198.

7. Ibid., p. 198.

8. *Presidential Control of Agency Rulemaking*, p. 10. See also Rosenberg, p. 198; and U.S. Senate, Committee on Environment and Public Works, *Executive Branch Review of Environmental Regulations*, Hearings before a subcommittee of the Committee on Environment and Public Works, 96th Cong., 1st sess., 1979.

9. Ibid.

10. Ibid., p. 10.

11. 3 C.F.R. 1971–1975 Comp., p. 926. The definition of a "major" rule was not precise.

12. Rosenberg, p. 199.

13. Ibid., p. 199.

14. 3 C.F.R. 1979 Comp., p. 1979.

15. Rosenberg, p. 199.

16. Ibid., p. 200–1.

17. U.S. Constitution, art. II, sec. 3.

18. U.S. Constitution, art. II, sec. 1.

19. Rosenberg, p. 220.

20. See ibid., pp. 219–33.

21. See Schick, *Congress and Money*, pp. 17–50.

22. See ibid., pp. 30–32; and Aaron Wildavsky, *The Politics of the Budgetary Process*, 2nd ed. (Boston: Little, Brown, 1974).

23. For a discussion of the short-term institutional, policy, and political effects of budgetary reform in Congress, see the essays in W. Thomas Wander, F. Ted Hebert, and Gary W. Copeland, eds., *Congressional Budgeting* (Baltimore: Johns Hopkins University Press, 1984).

24. McMurty, pp. 38–41.

25. It is difficult to overestimate the role of technology in advancing post-modern presidential budgetary prerogatives. It is safe to say that a significant lag in developing this technology (say, ten years) would have aborted the consolidation of post-modern budgetary prerogatives.

26. New York *Times*, December 6, 1986, p. 1, and December 19, 1986, p. 1.

27. *National Journal*, May 24, 1986, p. 1259.

28. 22 USC 2573 (1982).

29. Barilleaux, "Executive non-agreements," pp. 218–9.

30. Ibid., p. 219.

31. Ibid., p. 219.

32. Ibid., p. 220.

33. Ibid., p. 219.

34. 1 USC 112b (1982).

35. *Federal Register*, 13 July 1981, pp. 35917–21.

36. Ibid.

37. For a discussion of the Jackson Amendment and SALT I, see Ryan J. Barilleaux, *The President and Foreign Affairs: Evaluation, Performance, and Power* (New York: Praeger, 1985), pp. 73–94.

38. Some critics will contend that the modern presidency was already quite Hamiltonian in power. That argument is probably correct, but the post-modern presidency is more Hamiltonian. It operates in what is certainly more of an "administrative republic" than did the modern presidency. See Flaumenhauft, op. cit.

39. U.S. Congress, House, Committee on Rules, *Legislative Veto After Chadha*, hearings before the Committee on Rules, 98th Cong., 2nd sess., 1984, pp. 538–48.

40. Daniel Paul Franklin, "Why the legislative veto isn't dead," *Presidential Studies Quarterly* 16 (Summer 1986): 491–502.

5   *The Post-Modern Presidential Establishment*

Half a century ago, after surveying the sorry state of management assistance available to President Franklin Roosevelt, the President's Committee on Administrative Management concluded that "the President needs help."[1] Its recommendations stimulated the creation and growth of the Executive Office of the President, and U.S. government has never been the same since then.[2] Over the past half-century, the EOP has developed beyond its origins as an administrative support group, to become the general secretariat that post-modern presidents use to supervise and direct the work of the Executive Branch.

This presidential establishment occupies a central role in the operations of the contemporary Oval Office, so future chief executives must learn to manage and use it effectively. If they fail to do so, as did President Reagan in the Iran-Contra affair, their ability to govern will be jeopardized. On the other hand, presidents who can learn from Mr. Reagan's difficulties and other lessons of the post-modern presidential establishment will have the best chance of advancing their goals in the American system of shared governmental power.

What are those lessons? First, that the president must develop a strategy, before assuming office, for managing his general secretariat. Second, that presidents must abandon a number of persistent myths about Executive Branch management. Third, that the president needs a strong chief of staff, but not just any chief of staff. Finally, that senior presidential aides ought to be able to pass an exacting test intended to ensure that the president gets the kind of help he really needs.

Learning those lessons requires attention to the nature and role of the contemporary presidential establishment, how it functions and misfunctions, and how a president can make it work for him. A good starting point for these lessons is Mr. Reagan's Iran-Contra affair, because it reveals the perils of mismanaging the post-modern presidential establishment.

MR. REAGAN'S WHITE HOUSE MESS

For most of his tenure in the White House, Ronald Reagan projected an image of invincibility. Indeed, he was half-jokingly referred to as the "Teflon president" because mistakes and setbacks did not stick to him. He maintained an aura of success:[3] the public held him in high regard for his unflappable optimism, projection of American values, and ability to move public policy in the direction he wanted it to go. Even if he suffered setbacks in Beirut and the growing federal budget deficit, Mr. Reagan was widely credited with having proven that the presidency could still function as an effective force in American government.

Many of these impressions changed, however, when a series of revelations in the fall of 1986 disclosed secret U.S. arms sales to Iran, apparently in exchange for the release of Americans hostages held in Beirut, that were run by members of the National Security Council staff.[4] This affair was complicated by the fact that proceeds from the arms sales were funnelled to guerrilla forces—the "Contras"—fighting the Sandinista government of Nicaragua, apparently in violation of U.S. law.

This Iran-Contra affair became a scandal for Mr. Reagan's presidency.[5] The president's Assistant for National Security Affairs, Vice-Admiral John Poindexter, resigned because of his involvement. Lt. Colonel Oliver North, a Marine officer on the NSC staff who managed the arms sales, diversion of funds to the Contras, and secret Swiss bank accounts for the money, was fired. Accusations of wrongdoing or complicity in the affair were leveled against CIA Director William Casey, White House Chief of Staff Donald Regan, Attorney General Edwin Meese, Vice-President George Bush, and even President Reagan.[6]

Within a month of the story's initial disclosure, Mr. Reagan's public approval rating dropped about twenty-one points. By March of 1987, only forty-two percent of the American people approved of the president's performance in office.[7]

The result was a flurry of activity in the White House and Congress to dissect the affair. The president named a three-member panel of senior statesmen to investigate the affair (the Tower Commission), appointed a new NSC Adviser, and created a special working group to coordinate "responses to Congressional and other requests for information in a timely manner."[8] In Congress, special committees were formed in each house to investigate the affair, particularly the direction of covert activities by the ostensibly advisory staff of the NSC. An Independent Counsel was named to investigate the possibility of criminal charges arising from the arms sales, fund transfers, and related activities. Finally, Donald Regan, the president's chief of staff, was forced to resign and was replaced by former Senate Majority Leader Howard Baker. After the Tower Commission blamed the president for being too detached from the management of the affair, Mr. Reagan appeared on national television to apologize to the country. Unlike most waning second presidential terms, 1987 proved to be a busy year.

The affair was shocking for several reasons. First, the arms-for-hostages deal with Iran contradicted the Reagan Administration's stated policy of not bargaining with terrorists. Second, use of the NSC staff to manage these covert operations not only circumvented the Senate and Defense departments and the CIA, but probably violated several U.S. laws. Third, while President Reagan had authorized some exchange of arms for hostages, it became clear that he was ignorant of many important aspects of the affair until much later. Indeed, the Tower Commission report laid blame for the extent of the affair on the president and his senior advisors. Mr. Reagan had been too casual and removed from decision making in the affair to stay abreast of developments, but his staff had not compensated for the president's management style.[9] That fact validated critics' complaint that Mr. Reagan was too detached from the operations of the government, at least certain aspects of those workings.[10] Fourth, the clandestine handling of the affair by North and Poindexter, followed by turnover in senior presidential staff, revealed disarray in White House operations. It became clear that the Administration's image of a well-run White House was a false one. Finally, because these events and developments belied the president's reputation for political shrewdness, they suggested that Mr. Reagan could not keep his own house in order.

The mess that developed over the Iran-Contra affair weakened Mr. Reagan's presidency. It did not really affect his office as much as it affected his conduct of it. Ronald Reagan really had little left on his policy agenda for his last two years in office, so a scandal served to fill the political vacuum before the 1988 election. It also focused attention on the mess in the White House, thus deflecting eyes away from policy.

The scandal did not erase whatever mark Mr. Reagan had already made on his office, in the way of altering the political agenda or consolidating the post-modern presidency, but it did reveal the fragility of presidential influence. For the drop in his approval rating, the fact of his imminent departure from office and national attention to the scandal all served to diminish Mr. Reagan's ability to move events. He still had his prerogative power, certainly, but his effective at public politics was seriously weakened.

What did all of this mean for the presidency and future holders of the office? That question can only be answered by examining the post-modern presidential establishment and the president's management of it. The Iran-Contra affair is not important to the contemporary presidency because it is a second Watergate, but because it is a post-modern Bay of Pigs. A look at the president's general secretariat will reveal why that is so.

THE GENERAL SECRETARIAT AND THE POST-MODERN WHITE HOUSE

Mr. Reagan's general secretariat arose from the presidential establishment that has been developing since the time of FDR, and whose growth accelerated in the past two decades. Because presidents have long sought to make the Executive Branch responsive to their goals, policies, and priorities, they have tended to rely on the EOP to get the job done.

The basic issue fueling the rise and development of this general secretariat has been the competition between presidential control of the Executive Branch and bureaucratic autonomy. This competition results from the president's attempts to live up to his constitutional responsibilities as he sees them, to protect his electoral base or place in history, and to advance his policy goals. In these attempts he is often frustrated by the bureaucracy, which responds to congressional mandates and appropriations, a sense of mission, and interest group or issue network concerns.

The President, the Bureaucracy, and the General Secretariat

In nearly all aspects of executive politics in American government, from budgeting to rulemaking to program implementation, presidents have confronted the bureaucracy and used a variety of techniques to control it. Francis Rourke identified three general tactics presidents have employed in this regard: 1) "presidentializing" the executive bureaucracy (i.e., using appointments to take control of the senior levels of executives agencies); 2) White House monitoring of Executive Branch activities; and, 3) creating White House staff organizations to actually perform line-agency functions.[11]

In the post-modern presidency, the first two of these have been used extensively, with White House monitoring assuming a leading role. White House staff organizations are less common, although the NSC staff's role in the Iran-Contra affair was a notable exception.

All presidents want their appointees to advance administration goals and protect the interests of the Chief Executive, although some pay more attention to this tactic than do others. President Nixon did so, but encountered difficulties because of Watergate. Jimmy Carter did not begin with this device, but moved toward it as time passed. The most intensive use of the appointments strategy came with the inauguration of Ronald Reagan: as Richard Nathan put it, "The essence of the Reagan approach to management is the appointment of loyal and determined policy officials."[12]

Mr. Reagan used presidential appointment power to ensure that his nominees would advance his goals, not those of the bureaucracy or an issue network. Many of his choices were criticized for inexperience or even ignorance of the policy areas in their charge, but the president got what he wanted in the way of loyal officials.

More important to the post-modern presidency, however, has been the use of White House monitoring. Monitoring is certainly not a new idea, but the consolidation of certain presidential prerogatives has made it a more effective tool in recent years. For years, presidents employed budgetary systems (e.g., PPBS, MBO, ZBB) and other monitoring to oversee the work of the Executive Branch, but never with the degree of success they desired.[13] But the development of administrative clearance, legislative clearance, top-down budgeting, a domestic policy staff, and a generally stronger EOP have enabled the president to direct and supervise his branch of the government.

These developments, which are largely post-modern in nature, lie at the heart of the power of the president's general secretariat. They give the president, through the EOP, the ability to assert his goals and interests in policy formulation, budget making, regulation writing, and budget execution.

With these tools, the EOP has become a general secretariat. The president, however much his appointees may help him, need not rely on their loyalty to push the bureaucracy in the direction he wants it to go. He can use his secretariat for oversight. That does not mean that his troubles with the bureaucracy are over, but it does mean that the president can better advance his goals in several important aspects of administration. As a result, the Executive Branch of U.S. government has become more centralized than it was in the era of the modern presidency.

Less significant to post-modern presidents is the use of White House staff organizations for line functions. As the NSC staff's direction of covert activities in the Iran-Contra affair made clear, this tactic is potentially very dangerous for the president. It not only lacks legitimacy in the eyes of many observers, because it is clearly an attempt to circumvent established administrative channels rather than to supervise them, but it also encounters problems of illegality. In the era of the new Congress, which wants to exercise greater oversight of administration even if that goal is not always reached, the costs of using this tactic can be quite high.

The more effective tactic, then, has been White House monitoring. But to do it effectively presidents have had to develop the large Executive Office staff they now possess ("the swelling of the presidency"), seize political control of Executive Office units ("de-institutionalization"), and consolidate their new prerogatives. As with other aspects of the post-modern presidency, Ronald Reagan's general secretariat is built on the success and failures of past presidents.

The confluence of presidential needs with Executive Office capabilities and presidential prerogatives thus makes the general secretariat an important feature of the contemporary presidency. So future presidents will use this secretariat and must learn how to do so effectively.

Presiding Over the Executive Branch

Because the general secretariat has become a fixture of the contemporary presidency, the Chief Executive himself must learn to manage it and understand his role in the post-modern White House. If he does not, the president will find himself the victim of a staff that is beyond his control.

One key to this understanding is for the president to appreciate the fact that his general secretariat exists as a medium (happy or otherwise) between two alternative modes of presiding over the Executive Branch: the White House as "central chancery" and the White House as "clearinghouse." In the first mode, the president attempts to run all major functions of the executive out of the White House. This approach was essentially the one taken by Richard Nixon when he created certain policy "czars" (e.g., Henry Kissinger) who were both Cabinet secretaries and Assistants to the President for some broad areas of policy (national security, economic affairs). It certainly was not intended to delegate power to the Cabinet, but to centralize it in the White House. To that extent, the White House was to become (if the plan had succeeded) a sort of "central chancery" through which the Executive Branch would be run. This approach is politically controversial, however, for the same reasons that White House staff organizations performing line functions lack legitimacy.

The second mode has never really been used in modern times to the extent promised by a number of presidents, but it is important because it represents an ideal to which many recent presidents have pledged their fidelity. Specifically, it is the idea of "Cabinet government." In this mode, power resides in Cabinet departments and the White House acts as a "clearinghouse" to coordinate the various programs and agencies.

Like Hamlet's wassail, however, presidents have honored the notion of "Cabinet government" more in the breach than in the observance. Jimmy Carter and Ronald Reagan each pledged to allow their Cabinet secretaries broad power to administer their departments, formulate policy, implement programs, and enter the public debate on issues related to their portfolios, but neither lived up to that pledge. President Carter made an effort to allow his Cabinet members wide latitude, but was uncomfortable with their freedom and ultimately reduced it. President Reagan never really allowed the freedom he had advocated.

What Mr. Carter discovered and Mr. Reagan always seemed to know was that "Cabinet government" is inconsistent with assertive presidential policymaking. In order to advance his goals and interests, a president who wants to make his mark on government cannot allow his ministers the freedom promised by "Cabinet government."

So, between these two alternatives, recent presidents have developed a general secretariat that enables them to supervise and oversee the Executive Branch without drawing all major functions into the White House. By using the central clearance process (legislative and administrative), centralized budgeting, and Executive Office policy units (e.g., the National Security Council, Office of Policy Development, etc.), the president can advance his goals and control the Executive Branch without excessive centralization.[14] "Cabinet government" is unwieldy and counterproductive from the president's perspective, but a "central chancery" lacks legitimacy and engenders controversy.[15]

The general secretariat is a working compromise that serves presidential interests within the constraints of political acceptability. Cabinet members are not merely cyphers, but neither are they free agents. The president can allow them a certain latitude to float controversial proposals (e.g., tax overhaul, catastrophic health insurance), but keep the departments and agencies on some kind of leash. Because Executive Office capabilities and presidential prerogatives now match the needs of the Chief Executive, this secretariat will be an important feature of the presidency for a long time.

But it is no golden mean. Administrative clearance and top-down budgeting have been the subjects of extensive criticism, with the former subjected to challenges in court.[16] Moreover, having a general secretariat does not assure the president that it will always protect his interests. Finally, no secretariat, however well it does its job, can guarantee the president success in Congress, diplomacy, or public politics.

Running the Post-Modern White House

Once the president understands this compromise, he confronts the problem of actually running the White House. That task is not a small one, and it is fraught with a number of risks: paralysis in the policy process, bureaucratic revolt, or even a loss of control. To minimize those risks, the Chief Executive must accept several consequences of having a general secretariat.

1. A big and active presidential establishment is inevitable. Scholars, journalists, and even presidential candidates have lamented the "swelling of the presidency," but that swelling will not be reversed at any time in the near future. Because future presidents will want to maintain their ability to oversee budget construction, rulemaking, and policy formulation, as well as maintain contacts in Congress, interest groups, and the media, they will need the large presidential establishment that has developed in recent years. Moreover, that establishment exists as a conglomerate of offices and agencies. So, the president must approach his secretariat not in terms of sheer size, but in terms of drawing together its diverse components to serve his purposes.

2. Goodbye to the non-hierarchical White House. Perhaps the general secretariat's most significant consequence for presidential management (and theorizing about presidential management) is that it makes obsolete the ideal of a non-hierarchical White House staff. This ideal was cherished by John Kennedy and influenced many of his successors, who shared his idea that the president ought to be the "hub" around which all operations ought to revolve.[17] These presidents, including Jimmy Carter and Lyndon Johnson, feared the "bureaucratic" rigidity and presidential isolation of a hierarchical White House, which Kennedy and his advisors had disparaged in the Eisenhower Administration.[18]

But, as Carter discovered when he tried to emulate Kennedy, the White House and EOP of the 1970s had grown too large and complex to work effectively through a non-hierarchical or "collegial" management system. Whatever success President Kennedy may have had with a collegial system in his day was unachievable almost two decades later.[19] President Carter slowly introduced hierarchy into his White House and eventually even appointed a chief of staff.

With the general secretariat so large and so involved both in monitoring the Executive Branch and aiding the president, the Chief Executive must be able to deal with hierarchy and manage it. The price of an effective secretariat and presidential supervision of the executive is a more bureaucratic White House.

3. Goodbye to "Cabinet government." It is time to put to rest the myth of "Cabinet government." It is a myth because it has never really existed and because even those who process to believe in it are not quite sure if they do. But the myth remains, because the notion of strong, almost autonomous Cabinet secretaries has appeal in some political and scholarly circles, perhaps due to sentimental ideas about great ministers of state such as Jefferson, Hamilton, and John Quincy Adams. But even those men were careful about representing their presidents' interests. If the contemporary Chief Executive wants to make his mark on the government, he will ensure that his ministers do likewise, and their departments as well, and that means White House monitoring and not "Cabinet government."

4. Hello to a Chief of Staff. A corollary to the ideal of the non-hierarchical White House was the rejection of a presidential chief of staff. The idea of such a position carried with it connotations, at least to men such as John Kennedy, of military bureaucracy, palace guards, and isolated leaders. But in the post-modern White House, with its inevitable hierarchy, the president must have a chief of staff if he is not to be overwhelmed by the management aspects of his job. While the necessarily hierarchical White House is the most significant consequence of the general secretariat, its most important feature is the position of chief of staff.

THE PRESIDENT NEEDS A CHIEF OF STAFF

Scholars of the presidency have long emphasized the limits on presidential power,[20] but have implicitly assumed that the Chief Executive is omnicompetent. The president has been expected to provide political and moral leadership for the nation, excel at public politics and private diplomacy, move Congress, act as his own Secretary of State, manage the economy, and run the White House.[21] Indeed, one of the most common ways of teaching students about the office is to list and explain the many "hats" that a president must wear: Chief of State, Chief Executive, Leader of Public Opinion, Party Leader, and so on.[22] The list seems to grow longer with time, and seldom do its explicators consider the president's capacity to perform all of these functions.

Even if incumbents in the era of the modern presidency were capable of wearing all of these hats, post-modern presidents are not. The reason is not a decline in the quality of American statesmanship, but a change in the nature of the presidency. Now that the post-modern presidency has arrived, the occupant of the Oval Office needs the help of a chief assistant with power to direct the EOP.

Because the post-modern presidential establishment is big, complex, hierarchical, and powerful, it needs direction and leadership. Of course, the ideal person to provide those qualities is the president, but he is also called upon to wear many other "hats." The Chief Executive cannot delegate most of his other functions and responsibilities and, indeed, good management of the president's general secretariat is vital to their fulfillment. So the president needs management help most of all. Whereas no one else can make the ultimate decisions and stand for the president in his leadership roles, he can get help in keeping his own house in order.

Having a chief of staff is no panacea for the president's management needs, but it is the key to fulfilling them. The president's success at advancing his goals and meeting his responsibilities is built on his general secretariat, but he cannot be expected to manage it and do everything else all at once. He must delegate some power in this regard, and a chief of staff is the means for doing so.

For better or worse, the president needs a chief of staff. What future presidents must understand are the specific requirements of that job so they can fill it effectively.

Job Description for a White House Chief of Staff

One is tempted to write a pithy and sarcastic job advertisement for a prospective chief of staff:

Wanted: Person-Friday for chief executive of a large, dynamic, and growing North American republic. Duties include staff direction, backchannel negotiating, second-guessing of everything, protecting the boss' interests, and time management for the chief. Must have plenty of administrative and political experience, good Washington connections, thick skin, a passion for anonymity, willingness to work long hours and weekends, strong political instincts, and an endless capacity to say "no". Salary OK, benefits good, but perks include nice corner office, limo, and a chance to make things happen. Apply in person, 1600 Pennsylvania Avenue, Washington, D.C.

Of course, while the real job description for a presidential chief of staff is not too far from this mark, it is more involved and worthy of closer attention.

1. Responsibilities. The chief of staff's primary purpose is to direct the White House staff and the EOP. In this capacity, he is more than primus inter pares among senior presidential aides but less than Grand Vizier: his task is to relieve the president of most purely managerial aspects of running the presidential establishment. One of his most important responsibilities is overseeing the process of White House operations—politicking, policymaking, and internal functioning—in order to ensure that the president gets the kind of staff work he needs and is not surprised by what his aides are doing (or not doing) in his name.

The chief of staff must also be alert to protecting the president's political and institutional interests. That obligation may lead him to second-guess an ingenious staff plan to divert arms profits to the Contras or question the president's determination to make a lonely stand against Congress when compromise is possible. For the former task, the staff chief must be the president's eyes and ears. For the later one, he must sometimes be the president's conscience.

Finally, the chief of staff is responsible for preparing the president: to meet congressional leaders, to face a news conference, to make an important speech, to attend a summit. The chief of staff may not actually perform the requisite briefings himself, but he must see that they are done.

All of these duties combine to make a pair of very large shores to fill. But if the chief is to be useful to his boss, he must fill them. Therefore, he must possess certain abilities, qualifications, and experience that will see him through the demands of his position.

2. Prerequisite abilities. In order to be fit for the job, the chief of staff must be able to straddle the two major characteristics of White House operations: politics and administration. The presidential establishment is a bureaucratic conglomerate, made up of a number of subunits and agencies, so it needs effective management. But it is also a political bureaucracy, not just a public agency: it is engaged in advancing and defending political causes, promoting the political interests of a specific politician, and dealing with other formal and informal institutions. The White House is not merely another bureaucracy or big business enterprise on Pennsylvania Avenue. It is a political establishment.

Therefore, the chief of staff must be competent at administering a highly visible political organization. He must possess the sound political judgment and sensitivities that come with experience, as well as a willingness to subordinate his own personal ambitions to those of the president. Without these abilities, the Chief will be more a burden to the president than a source of help.

3. Qualifications/experience. If the president wants to derive maximum benefit from his staff chief, he must appoint one with more qualifications than loyalty to the boss. He must find a chief who will contribute to the president's professional reputation.

The chief of staff must possess a record of high-level political responsibility sufficient to warrant appointment to a quasi-Cabinet-level post. Without this record, he will need long and politically expensive on-the-job training, make too many mistakes, and weaken the president. A contrast between Ronald Reagan's first and second staff chiefs demonstrates this point: the first, James Baker, had a long and distinguished record, so he was able immediately to put the Reagan White House in order and achieve important victories for the president; the second, Donald Regan, lacked Baker's experience and failed to protect his boss' interests in the Iran-Contra affair. Mr. Reagan's third chief of staff, Howard Baker, was a political expert who demonstrated the sorts of skills his job demanded.

He must also possess a reputation sufficient to engender confidence in him in Congress and the rest of the Washington community. His appointment ought therefore to elicit cries of "Of course" rather than "Who?" When Jimmy Carter finally put Hamilton Jordan in charge of his staff in 1978, Jordan's Washington reputation was only two years old and almost exclusively negative. His appointment did little for the Carter Administration except to suggest to many observers that Mr. Carter's presidency was collapsing. In contrast, the appointment of Howard Baker, highly regarded in Congress, was greeted with universal praise on Capitol Hill. That fact helped restore some confidence in Ronald Reagan's presidency.

Finally, a chief of staff ought to possess experience with more than one political leader. This experience will enable him to offer the president a broader perspective on how things are done in politics, as well as give the staff chief a larger picture of political life than one leader can provide. H.R. Haldeman and Hamilton Jordan, staff chiefs to presidents in trouble whom many observers believed made their bosses' problems worse,[23] each had a career limited to the service of a single political leader. A broader perspective will not make a staff chief invulnerable, but a limited perspective ensures the president a chief aide whose experience is no better than his own.

The appointment of his Chief of Staff presents a president with the opportunity to supplement his own abilities and experience. That is why loyalty to the boss is but one qualification for the job. Because the chief of staff is a prominent and important position in any administration, the incumbent in that job ought to add to the president's aura of competence, not just bask in it.

The Chief of Staff Is Not Deputy President

As important as a chief of staff is to the success of the post-modern presidency, the position is not that of "deputy president." The chief ought not and cannot be the only conduit to the president, because then the boss is truly isolated. Nor can the chief of staff relieve the president of his obligation to keep his own house in order. Power can be delegated, but responsibility cannot. The American system provides for the executive power to reside in one person, so the president must keep his staff chief on a leash.

THE ROLE OF THE VICE-PRESIDENT

Perhaps the most tenuous aspect of the post-modern presidency is the new vice-presidency. The last three vice presidents, Nelson Rockefeller, Walter Mondale, and George Bush, have occupied a position transformed: once the butt of jokes, the vice-presidency has assumed an important place in the White House in recent years.

How does it fit into the post-modern presidential establishment? Mondale and Bush each seems to have found his niche as a senior presidential counselor without portfolio, that is, without specific duties. Both took temporary assignments to work on projects that would advance administration goals—Mondale, the SALT II Task Force and Bush, the Task Force on Regulatory Relief—but neither attempted to act as another Assistant to the President.[24] In this way, each was able to remain somewhat above the fray of White House politics and offer the president some sage advice.

In the post-modern White House, this role could grow even more valuable to the harried Chief Executive. The increasing demands on presidential time and attention that make a chief of staff necessary also favor an activist vice-president. The Second Citizen can offer the First the benefit of his knowledge of national issues, the policy process, and political strategy, all within the context of an administration loyalist whose own reputation is affected by that of the boss.

Of course, vice-presidents and the White House staff have long been regarded as natural enemies, because the president's aides are often suspicious of this stranger carrying on in the name of the administration. Lyndon Johnson was the victim of such suspicion as John Kennedy's second, and Spiro Agnew was the victim of Richard Nixon's aides.[25] What, then, has caused the situation to change?

First, tradition, so important to the American presidency, is developing in support of an activist vice-president. Three vice-presidents in a row are distinguishable from nearly all of their predecessors in importance, so future Second Citizens will have precedent on their side. The vice-president now possesses a White House office, a substantial staff, and regular access to the president.[26] Second, the opening of the presidential nominating field to Washington "outsiders" means that "insiders" are natural for ticket-balancing and then helping the president succeed in the capital. Third, the various changes in the political environment that have helped alter the presidency—the new political agenda, changes in Congress, the new electoral politics—also mean that contemporary presidents do not have the same circle of party and congressional advisors their predecessors relied upon.[27] So the vice-president is a potentially valuable source of advice. The Second Citizen usually has more political experience than most of the president's aides, as well as the successful record in politics that attracted the presidential candidate to this running mate.

Therefore, post-modern presidents will likely keep the new vice-presidency. Of course, that decision ultimately rests with each pair of First and Second Citizens. But with a big and active presidential establishment to operate, a new political environment all around, and the need for all the help they can get, future presidents will want to take advantage of that senior politician whose political fate is most closely tied to their own.

MR. REAGAN'S BAY OF PIGS

Revelations about the Iran-Contra affair punctured President Reagan's well-constructed image of handling his responsibilities with almost effortless skill. They exposed him not only to the vicissitudes of public opinion, but also to sharp criticisms from his allies and opponents alike. What the affair did to Mr. Reagan's tenure was to embroil him in the sort of scandal that damages an incumbent's professional reputation and encourages pundits to wonder out loud about the wisdom of the American presidential institution.

Like any major negative headline, this affair invited comparison with other scandals in White House history. Some observers saw parallels between the Iran-Contra affair and Watergate, because of secret transfers of money, the possibility of widespread lying among senior government officials, and attempts to conceal these activities from Congress and the public.[28] But such comparisons were wrong, because the Iran-Contra affair really was more a post-modern Bay of Pigs than a second Watergate.

The Bay of Pigs affair was the 1961 incident in which the Kennedy Administration met with humiliation and defeat in its attempt to manage an assault by Cuban exiles on Castro's Cuba. In that affair, presidential mismanagement of decision making processes was an important factor that led to the disaster.[29]

The Iran-Contra affair was Mr. Reagan's Bay of Pigs for several reasons. First, it was in essence the failure of a secret foreign-policy initiative that occurred because of a breakdown in presidential decision making, and which was a badly flawed idea from its inception. That characterization also applies to the Bay of Pigs. Second, the motive behind both the Iran-Contra affair and the Bay of Pigs was to make a breakthrough on a foreign-policy problem sticking like a thorn in the administration's side (i.e., Castro, and American hostages in Beirut). In Watergate, the motives were base. As Arthur Schlesinger has put it, "The Watergate mob was out to destroy political opposition; the current crowd is out to save the world."[30] Finally, an important reason for the fiascoes in 1961 and 1986 was that Presidents Kennedy and Reagan each failed to live up to his responsibilities in managing policymaking and execution.[31]

But the Iran-Contra affair is no mere replay of the Bay of Pigs, and the comparison cannot be pushed too far. The essential point, however, is that a guide to understanding this mess is not to be found in Watergate. Rather, the cast of the Bay of Pigs can suggest some points for analysis.

Specifically, the Bay of Pigs case suggests that the roots of the Iran-Contra affair be sought in White House operations and presidential management.[32] But Iran-Contra came a quarter of a century later, so other factors are also important: the role of the president's chief of staff, the operating style of the president involved, and the specific experiences and goals of the Reagan Administration.

White House Operations

The Iran-Contra affair occurred, at least in part, because of problems in the management and operations of the presidential establishment. Specifically, President Reagan and his chief of staff short-circuited normal policy processes for foreign policy to conduct the Iran arms deals, and the attendant transfer of funds to the Contras, from the White House itself.

President Reagan had originally constructed his foreign-policy decision apparatus to include strong secretaries of State and Defense. Indeed, his first National Security Advisor, Richard Allen, reported to the president through the Counselor to the president. Unlike the Nixon–Kissinger NSC system, which was designed to shut the two national security departments out of decision making, Mr. Reagan's system was more traditional: a State–Defense–NSC troika. In the Iran-Contra affair, however, policymaking and execution were kept in the White House (with some CIA involvement). Because they strongly opposed arms deals with Iran, the secretaries of State and Defense were excluded from most policymaking on that issue. The effect of that move was to deny the president the advice or knowledge of two of his senior subordinates. By closing the advisory circle, the president, his staff chief, and National Security Advisor weakened the decision-making process.

A second aspect of operations that reveals mismanagement was in the secret fund diversion to the Contras. Colonel North was running a series of Swiss bank accounts and other activities apparently without the knowledge of the president or the White House chief of staff. What else might have gone on without their knowledge? Here is a clear example of neither the president nor his chief aide being able to keep the White House in order. If the general secretariat can act unilaterally, it can quickly become a "loose cannon." It's no surprise that the whole affair blew up in Mr. Reagan's face.

The problem is closely tied to the use of the NSC staff for managing covert operations. Not only does this action violate the political, bureaucratic, and possibly legal authority of the NSC staff, but it is a mistake. As noted above, using White House staff units for line functions is politically risky and often more trouble than it is worth. In this case, the NSC-run operations raised the possibility of further restrictions on covert operations and closer congressional scrutiny of the National Security Council. In the end, the result of using the NSC staff in this way was to weaken the president's ability to act.

Finally, the crux of the problems in White House operations was the chief of staff. It was his responsibility to help the president keep the general secretariat under control, to guard the president's political interests, and to facilitate effective decision making. Unfortunately, Donald Regan did none of these things. On his watch as staff chief, the NSC staff conducted illegal operations that were hidden from the president and possibly Mr. Regan himself.[33] The chief of staff failed to protect the president's interests by not fighting the Iran arms deal, which ultimately cost Mr. Regan dearly and earned him little credit. Then, when the affair became public knowledge, Mr. Regan sent the president before reporters with insufficient briefing on the matter.[34] Finally, he helped shut the secretaries of State and Defense out of the foreign-policy decision process, thus inhibiting policy effectiveness.

In all, he did not live up to his responsibilities as chief of staff. As the Tower Commission put it,

Mr. Regan also shares in this responsibility. More than almost any chief of staff in recent memory, he asserted personal control over the White House staff and sought to extend his control to the national security adviser. He was personally active in national security affairs and attended almost all the relevant meetings regarding the Iran initiative. He, as much as anyone, should have insisted that an orderly process be observed. In addition, he especially should have ensured that plans were made for handling any public disclosure of the initiative. He must bear primary responsibility for the chaos that descended upon the White House when such disclosures did occur.[35]

So, the affair stems in some large part from these operational failings. But those problems were accompanied by others.

The President and His Surrogates

In one sense, the Iran-Contra affair could be called "Surro-gate," because one of its root causes was the president's excessive delegation of power to his staff. The president allocated broad power to his surrogates in the Executive Office, and they brought him trouble. As Theodore Draper has commented, this affair is about more than what the president himself knew or authorized: "It is a crisis not only about what president has the power to do; it is also about the power of those around him or behind him to act in his name."[36] Mr. Reagan not only focused on the "big picture" of foreign policy to the exclusion of important details, but effectively detached himself from White House operations.

Mr. Reagan's detachment is seen in his lack of knowledge about exactly what went on in the Iran-Contra affair. He certainly was not entirely ignorant of his own house to be surprised when many revelations about the affair were made in late 1986.

The Tower Commission noted Mr. Reagan's detachment, the failure of responsibility such distance involved, and the consequences of his removal. The Commission concluded that "the President did not seem to be aware of the way in which the operation was implemented and the full consequences of U.S. participation."[37] Furthermore, there is no substitute for presidential attentiveness:

the President should have insured that the NSC system did not fail him. He did not force his policy to undergo the most critical review of which the NSC participants and the process were capable. At no time did he insist upon accountability and performance review. Had the President chosen to drive the NSC system, the outcome could well have been different. As it was, the most powerful features of the NSC system—providing comprehensive analysis, alternatives and follow-up—were not utilized.[38]

Mr. Reagan delegated too much power to his staff and failed to immerse himself sufficiently in the details of policy to protect his own interests. He remained unfamiliar with many important aspects of this potentially explosive policy, despite the fact that it was all run out of the White House.

Perhaps the source of this detachment is the problem of "negative learning" on President Reagan's part. "Negative learning" refers to the president's learning the wrong lessons from his experience in office. Specifically, the experience of his first term apparently led Mr. Reagan to conclude that he need not pay close attention to his duties in order to handle the responsibilities of his office.

In the first Reagan Administration, the president operated essentially as "chairman of the board," leaving the details White House operations and policy to a small group of senior aides: Chief of Staff James Baker, Deputy Chief of Staff Michael Deaver, Counselor to the President Edwin Meese, and the National Security Advisor (first William Clark and then Robert McFarlane).[39] He was able to take this course because his senior aides were astute and experienced at protecting his political and policy interests, and especially because of the abilities of the chief of staff. James Baker was the sort of staff leader Ronald Reagan needed: he possessed the necessary of combination of political and administrative experience, was a skilled bargainer, and had the necessary judgment to know how much detail the president needed in order to function effectively. With Baker's help, Mr. Reagan was able to focus on the "big picture" quite effectively, use his talents at public politics, achieve a number of his policy goals, and avoid any serious political damage from setbacks and problems.[40]

In the second Reagan Administration, the president used a somewhat different organizational scheme. Deaver and McFarlane had left government service, while Baker and Meese were now in Cabinet posts. So the president, apparently believing that his "chairmanship" could be carried further in the second term, named Donald Regan to be chief of staff. There were no other senior aides with status comparable to that of Meese and Deaver, so all staff power essentially flowed through Regan. This move allowed the president to detach himself further from the details of governing, because the staff chief could now act as the president's surrogate. But Donald Regan lacked Baker's political experience and, as Wicker's comment illustrates, Baker's abilities. The result was a decline in the quality of White House management from the first administration to the second.

Paul Light has argued that one feature of presidential governing is the "cycle of increasing effectiveness," that is, the president and his staff tend to get better at their jobs as they gain experience in office.[41] But this trend of rising effectiveness was neutralized and reversed by Mr. Reagan's "negative learning": the president apparently concluded, on the basis of his system in the first term, that he could empower a very strong chief of staff to run the White House for him.

Of course, President Reagan was not completely out of touch with his staff, as some of his critics have claimed, but he was sufficiently detached from its management to be at the mercy of his staff chief's abilities and shortcomings. Donald Regan did not perform as required, so the president became embroiled in a scandal big enough to penetrate his image of effectiveness and jeopardize some of his policy goals.

Right and Wrong Lessons

If the Iran-Contra affair is to have any meaning for the presidency, it is important that presidents and pundits draw the right lessons from this post-modern Bay of Pigs. Otherwise, the affair will serve only as the basis for overreaction and misunderstanding of three important issues.

1. Delegation by the president. Because delegation was a problem at the heart of this affair, it is vital to the office that future presidents do not overreact to this issue. The Iran-Contra affair has not proven that a chief of staff is a bad idea; rather, it has highlighted the need for balance in delegation.

The last two presidents present a stark contrast on the issue of delegation: Jimmy Carter delegated far too little and Ronald Reagan far too much. Clearly, a balance must be struck. As the analysis above suggests, post-modern presidents need a chief of staff in order to avoid being overwhelmed by their responsibilities. Jimmy Carter learned this lesson to some extent and ultimately appointed a staff chief. But that does not mean that a president can rely on a surrogate to do his job. To repeat, the chief of staff is not Deputy President, and there is no substitute for a president looking out for himself.

The worst overreaction to Iran-Contra would be for observers to conclude that it proves that a president ought not have a staff chief. Kennedy had no chief of staff and still fell victim to the Bay of Pigs.

The need for a chief outweighs the problems. The challenge for the president is to balance the amount of power he delegates to that aide. That can be accomplished by the president's choosing the right kind of person to serve as staff chief, viewing that officer as the top aide to the president but not the only senior aide, and keeping enough of a hand in details to be familiar with important policy initiatives and assertions of presidential power.

2. *Negative learning and presidential management.* How can a president avoid the pitfalls of negative learning? There are no easy answers. Some observers have suggested close consultations with congressional leaders, others the creation of a permanent secretariat in the White House to serve as "institutional memory." Still others have counseled changes in the office or personality tests for presidential candidates.

All of these suggestions face the problem that the president must be willing to listen and learn if any advice or institutional memory is to be valuable. There's the rub. So, how can a president make himself open to advice? Ultimately, only the president's knowledge of his predecessors' problems will open his mind.

But there are other ideas beyond a sense of history that might give a president practical help. For example, a simple rule of thumb in choosing and directing senior aides could help ensure that the president gets the kind of help he needs and guard against negative learning. That is what might be called the "Rule of Defensibility": the president must choose each of his senior aides (say, anyone with rank of Assistant to the President) as if that officer's appointment depended on Senate confirmation; furthermore, the president and his aides must ensure that whatever they do can bear congressional scrutiny. If they follow this rule, then they will be less inclined to fall into the sort of trap that the Reagan Administration did in the Iran-Contra affair. As Watergate and Iran-Contra have shown, despite any protestations of executive privilege, there is little of White House operations that might not one day be brought before Congress. If the president were to follow this rule, he would probably be more inclined to avoid the problems of detachment and negative learning. Whatever and whomever cannot be defended in a congressional investigation is not worth the president's trouble. More than a permanent staff to provide institutional memory or polite visits with congressional leaders, this rule will keep the president and his establishment on the trend of rising effectiveness.

3. *Responsibility and blame.* A final issue arising from Iran-Contra is the question of responsibility for the affair. Who is to blame and who

should take the blame? That question can be answered only by distinguishing levels of responsibility.

Specifically, in the matter of executive policymaking, there are two levels of responsibility. First, primary responsibility lies with the president alone. He is the one elected to be Chief Executive and charged by the Constitution with specific powers and duties. He can delegate some of his power, but none of his democratic and constitutional responsibilities.

The president appointed the officers who conducted the Iran-Contra operations, and was thus responsible for their performance. Moreover, he was charged with taking care that the laws be faithfully executed. Finally, he was ultimately responsible for whatever was done in his name, even if he were unaware of it.

To that extent, President Reagan was responsible for the Iran-Contra affair. That is not to say that it was all his fault, but that he bears responsibility for it. Accordingly, his supporters' pleas for the president to publicly assume responsibility for the affair before the nation were very much in order.[42] Representative Henry Hyde, a strong supporter of Mr. Reagan, put the case for presidential responsibility in these terms:

If the president wants credit for the good things that have happened on his watch, he can't decline responsibility for errors and mistakes. . . . You had a risky foreign policy conducted by amateurs and that's the President's fault.[43]

John Kennedy understood this responsibility as well. After the Bay of Pigs disaster, Kennedy took responsibility for what had happened. He was perplexed when his public opinion ratings soared. But, by accepting responsibility, he demonstrated an understanding of both sides of the notion of presidential leadership, power and responsibility.

Mr. Reagan was not, however, alone in the White House. He had a number of subordinates involved in the affair, and they all bear secondary responsibility. Secondary responsibility is not less important, but it does not have the magnitude of the president's democratic and constitutional responsibility.

Admiral Poindexter and Colonel North became the most visible figures in the affair bearing responsibility, but others bore it as well. Specifically, Donald Regan bore responsibility for his failure to live up to the requirements of his job as staff chief, thus facilitating the president's slide into scandal. That failure earned him some responsibility for the affair and was evidence in favor of his dismissal.

Of course, President Reagan resisted firing his chief of staff, just as he resisted taking responsibility for the whole affair.[44] After the Bay of Pigs, Kennedy summoned CIA Director Allen Dulles into the Oval Office and told him something to the effect that "if this were Britain, I would have to go; but this is America, so you have to go." Dulles was fired, because a change in CIA directors is much less traumatic for the political system than the resignation of a president. When, ultimately, Mr. Regan was replaced by Howard Baker, the move came rather late and only gave the president partial credit for retaking charge of his administration. Although Mr. Reagan ultimately assumed responsibility for the affair, his delay in doing so seriously damaged his public credibility.

While bearing the ultimate responsibility for the Iran-Contra affair, Mr. Reagan should have sent his chief of staff packing early in the affair. By doing so, he would have helped to retire the controversy, removed one important source of his problems, and punished a subordinate for failure to perform effectively. This scandal was not sufficient to unseat a president, as some of the more intemperate observers suggested, but it did demand a house cleaning in the upper levels of the administration. By waiting so long to get a new staff chief, the president diminished confidence in his own abilities.

In this regard, the right lesson from Iran-Contra is that the president can never delegate ultimate responsibility. The wrong lesson is that he alone must take the blame. The various levels of responsibility and blame must be meted out properly.

IMPLICATIONS FOR FUTURE PRESIDENTS

The presidential establishment has come a long way from its somewhat humble beginnings in the 1930s. It has developed into a general secretariat through which the president governs, includes a new vice-presidency that is far more active than the old one, and can no longer operate as a non-hierarchical coterie of presidential assistants. The swelling of the presidential establishment has made it more bureaucratic, so it needs a chief of staff at the top to keep the First Citizen from being overwhelmed with his job.

The establishment's growth in size and importance means that the president must face the problem of internal White House management before he can face his other responsibilities. Accordingly, this chapter suggests several managerial prescriptions for future presidents who want to get on with the business of government.

First, a new president, before assuming office, must develop a strategy for operating and controlling his general secretariat. One key to this strategy is a strong chief of staff who can meet the demands outlined above, but who is not vested with such preeminence that he (or she) becomes "Deputy President." Rather, the president ought to make his staff chief first among a small group of senior aides, able to manage the White House staff but unable to isolate the boss.

Along with this strategy, the incoming president must decide on a role for his vice-president. As demonstrated above, that role is likely to be an active one, but only if the First Citizen chooses to make it so.

Related to this strategy is the second prescription for future presidential management: incoming leaders must abandon some myths of executive government. One myth is the dream of Cabinet government, which is an unrealized goal that ought to be doubted anyway. Why is Cabinet government such an attractive idea? It suggests disjointed policymaking and centrifugal government. Anyway, it won't work.

Conversely, the president cannot expect to run all of the government out of the White House. It is politically risky to do so, because of the bureaucratic and congressional resistance that approach stimulates. It is also dangerous from a management point of view. As the Iran-Contra affair demonstrated, the White House staff is not capable of effective unilateral action. It lacks both the experience and the expertise necessary for such action. The president must learn to use the EOP to oversee and manage the Executive Branch, not replace it.

Another myth is the ideal of the collegial White House, with no hierarchy and the president the "hub" of a policymaking "wheel." The big and active EOP makes that ideal a mistaken one. Future presidents must learn to work in hierarchical systems of some sort, or else be the victims of their own executive establishment.

Finally, future presidents ought to select and supervise senior aides according to the "Rules of Defensibility." Any officer with the rank of Assistant to the President ought to be appointed and supervised as if his appointment required Senate confirmation and thus congressional scrutiny. If this rule is followed, then presidential assistants and their actions will likely be defensible before Congress and the nation.

If a president enforces this rule on appointing senior aides, he is more likely to get the kind of help he really needs. Candidates for senior staff positions will be qualified for their jobs and command respect in Congress. They will possess both the political experience and the political skill necessary to serve the Chief Executive effectively.

A second reason for future presidents to follow this rule is that appointees qualifying according to its strictures are likely to have friends on Capitol Hill and in the press corps. These connections may mean that they are not solely creatures of the president, but they will be able to help him succeed with the "powers that be" in Washington.

A final reason for enforcing the Rule of Defensibility is reality. Although a president's assistants are his own, Richard Nixon and Ronald Reagan discovered that these aides can be called before Congress if the legislature so desires. Invoking executive privilege is no defense, because it smacks of hidden guilt. If senior aides or their actions cannot stand up under congressional scrutiny, then the president does not need that kind of help.

The Rule of Defensibility, if enforced by the president, will ultimately spread its effects throughout the presidential establishment. That result could only help the president, his office, and the political system.

These prescriptions are intended to enhance a president's ability to survive in the realm of executive politics. The contemporary presidential establishment needs careful and thoughtful management by the Chief Executive, so presidents who exhibit these administrative virtues will be the ones most likely to advance their goals in the post-modern era.

NOTES

1. U.S. President, President's Committee on Administrative Management, *Administrative Management in the Government of the United States* (Washington: Government Printing Office, 1937).

2. *Public Administration Times*, January 1, 1987, pp. 1–3.

3. For a discussion of this phenomenon, see Bruce Buchanan, *The Citizen's Presidency* (Washington: Congressional Quarterly Press, 1986), pp. 75–100.

4. At the time of the writing of this work (early 1987), much information about the Iran-Contra affair still had not been made public. Consequently, the analysis herein is constrained by the information available at the time. Nevertheless, it is possible to make many significant points about presidential management of the "general secretariat." For one thing about the whole affair is clear: it was not the result of careful, premeditated action by the president and

his subordinates, but involved a number of mistakes, misjudgments, and failures of White House policymaking.

5. No satisfactory name has been attached to the affair, so the one used here will be sufficient.

6. The affair was covered intensively by the news media and specific details can be found in any major newspaper or news magazine of the period from November 1986 on. The author's capsule summary of the affair, which is all that the limits of this work will allow, is drawn from coverage of the affair by the New York *Times*.

7. New York *Times*, December 7, 1986, sec. 4, p. 1; and March 2, 1987, p. 1.

8. New York *Times*, December 27, 1986, p. 1.

9. New York *Times*, February 27, 1987, p. 1. The *Times* printed excerpts from the report. For the entire report, see U.S. President, Special Review board, *Report of the President's Special Review Board*, February 26, 1987 (Washington: G.P.O., 1987).

10. Ibid., January 8, 1987, pp. 1 and 4.

11. Francis E. Rourke, "The Presidency and the bureaucracy," in *The Presidency and the Political System*, pp. 339–62, edited by Michael Nelson (Washington: Congressional Quarterly Press, 1984).

12. Nathan, p. 74.

13. See Wildavsky, *The Politics of the Budgetary Process*. Planning, Programming, Budgeting System (PPBS) was begun under Kennedy and expanded under Johnson. Nixon replaced PPBS with the Management by Objective (MBO) system. Carter employed Zero-Based Budgeting (ZBB). None of these devices worked as intended.

14. See Newland, "Executive Office policy apparatus," loc. cit.

15. See Argyle and Barilleaux, op. cit.

16. *Office of Management and Budget Influence on Agency Regulations*, pp. vii–viii.

17. Ryan J. Barilleaux, "Kennedy, the Bay of Pigs, and the limits of collegial decisionmaking," in *The Presidency and National Security Policy*, pp. 207–22, edited by R. Gordon Hoxie (New York: Center for the Study of the Presidency, 1984).

18. Disparaged on the basis of a misunderstanding of Eisenhower's management system. See Phillip G. Henderson, "Advice and decision: The Eisenhower National Security Policy reappraised," in *The Presidency and National Security Policy*, pp. 153–86, edited by R. Gordon Hoxie (New York: Center for the Study of the Presidency, 1984).

19. Kennedy's "success" with the collegial system is often overrated. See Barilleaux, "Kennedy," loc. cit.

20. This emphasis comes from what might be called the "Neustadt school"

of presidency studies. See Neustadt; Greenstein, "Change and Continuity;" and Hargrove and Nelson, Chapter 1.

21. Thomas Cronin has written eloquently on the paradoxes of the presidency, which this statement reflects. See his *The State of the Presidency*, 2nd ed. (Boston: Little, Brown, 1980).

22. This "hats" metaphor can be found in nearly any introductory American government college textbook and most high school civics books as well. It originated with Clinton Rossiter, *The American Presidency*, 2nd ed. (New York: Time, Inc., 1963).

23. Haldeman was widely regarded as isolating Nixon, while Jordan's behavior before and after becoming Chief of Staff damaged Carter's reputation. The point here is that the Chief of Staff's reputation, as well as performance, count.

24. Light, op. cit.

25. Ibid.

26. Ibid., p. 2.

27. For a similar point, see ibid., p. 259.

28. While the scandal revelations were coming to light in late 1986 and early 1987, most observers hesitated to openly call the affair a second Watergate. That claim, however, was frequently made in passing or obtusely. For illumination, see Arthur Schlesinger, Jr., "Why not question the Presidency?" New York *Times*, January 2, 1987, p. 25; and, William Safire, "Only a Bag of Pigs," New York *Times*, November 27, 1986, p. 27.

29. The Bay of Pigs affair is the subject of much investigation and controversy. An introduction to it can be found in Ryan J. Barilleaux, "Kennedy, the Bay of Pigs, and the limits of collegial decisionmaking," loc. cit. A well-known but flawed analysis is in Irving Janis, *Victims of Groupthink* (Boston: Houghton Mifflin, 1972). The most thorough journalistic account of the affair is Peter Wyden, *Bay of Pigs* (New York: Simon and Schuster, 1979).

30. Schlesinger, loc. cit.

31. On Kennedy's failings, see Barilleaux, "Kennedy," p. 219. On Reagan's failings, see the Tower Commission report or excerpts from it in New York *Times*, February 27, 1987, p. 1.

32. See ibid., pp. 210–217.

33. See New York *Times* throughout November and December, 1986, but specifically December 8, 1986, p. 1; November 26, 1986, p. 1; and December 5, 1986, p. 1. See also Richard Moe, "Taming the N.S.C.," New York *Times*, November 26, 1986, p. 27.

34. Tom Wicker, "Questions and some answers," New York *Times*, December 19, 1986, p. 31.

35. Ibid.

36. Theodore Draper, "Reagan's junta," *New York Review of Books*, January 29, 1987, p. 5.

37. New York *Times*, February 27, 1987, p. 16.

38. I previously defended Mr. Reagan's "chairman of the board," "big picture" approach to presidential management (see Argyle and Barilleaux, op. cit.). Those arguments still stand, but Mr. Reagan took his chairman's role too far: the president as overall policy director must not be too detached, but focus on the "big picture." To fail to keep an eye on important details is to fail to govern effectively.

39. In the first year of the first term, only Baker, Meese, and Deaver (the "troika") constituted this inner circle. After the departure of Richard Allen and the upgrading of the NSC in the White House organizational chart, the National Security Advisor became part of the circle of power (the "quadriad").

40. Some observers, such as one of my colleagues, have attributed Mr. Reagan's first-term successes and lack of serious failures to his great good luck. I doubt that anyone, especially a president, has that much luck.

41. Paul Light, *The President's Agenda* (Baltimore: Johns Hopkins University Press, 1982).

42. New York *Times*, January 15, 1987, pp. 1 and 4.

43. Ibid.

44. Ibid., p. 4.

6 *The Eye of the Beholder*

The post-modern president is not merely a creature of the White House, but appears regularly in livingrooms across the nation. Contemporary presidents tend to "go public" much more frequently than their predecessors ever did, so they are in the public eye more than earlier incumbents.

What does this development imply for the person in the Oval Office? It means that incumbents must deal with the media as both a conduit for public politics and an independent force in politics. Presidents will therefore attempt to control their exposure in the media: what television and print journalism show of them in photographs, what words of the president they transmit, and what questions and criticisms the president answers.

The post-modern presidency thus presents a new paradox for the office: it is more visible yet less accessible than its forerunners.[1] Presidents want to be seen, in order to get their message to the public, but they want to be seen on their own terms. So they try to set the rules and conditions for media coverage.

Such control presents a special challenge for journalists in particular and citizens in general. Journalists want to convey the news to their audience, but to do so according to their own judgment of how stories are to be told. Presidential control of the presidential image restricts reporters' ability to do so.

At the same time, citizens must receive the information coming from the White House, whether on the president's terms or the journalists', and use it to form opinions and evaluate the president. Citizens in the post-modern era also face a significant challenge, then, as they attempt to digest this information and use it to exercise their democratic responsibility as voters.

Consequently, the conjunction of public politics and the media age makes it harder for everyone involved—president, journalist, citizen—to live up to his or her responsibilities in a democracy. As this chapter will make clear, there are no quick and easy solutions to the challenges these developments produce.

A MORE VISIBLE PRESIDENCY

Because the political environment of the presidency has changed, presidential tactics for governing have also changed. Over the past two decades, presidents have pushed to extend their prerogative powers, increase their control over the Executive Branch, and use public politics to move the machinery of government. This last trend, that of "going public," has made the presidency a more visible institution.

Even without the use of public politics, television made the presidency more visible to citizens. Indeed, the presidency is that part of American politics best suited for television. The television camera captures individuals better than panoramic scenes, and is quite unable to show processes or institutions. How does one photograph a political party, interest group, or governmental agency, except through their representatives (or a building)? The president is his own best representative and daily more significant than a party or part of the bureaucracy. Moreover, the president deals in crisis, diplomacy, national symbols, and grand ideals, while others deal in paperwork, electioneering, and lobbying. With these factors encouraging a focus on the president, plus congressional reluctance to allow cameras in legislative chambers, the president in the 1960s became a television star.

Presidents also saw the value of television for delivering their message to voters. John Kennedy allowed the televising of his press conferences and used television addresses to stimulate public interest in his goals and policies. A rhetorically-minded incumbent, he showed how television could extend Wilson's notion of the rhetorical presidency. That lesson was not lost on his successors, and since Richard Nixon there has been a tendency for presidents to "go public" in order to promote their goals.

Television makes it easy for the president to use public politics, and not only because he can reach millions easily. As commander-in-chief, Leader of the Free World, manager of the economy, and so many other things, the president is news. He is easy to photograph and, according to journalists, worth photographing. By a simple request, he can obtain free time during prime viewing hours on all three major commercial networks. The president need expend only a little effort to be highly visible.

With a new political environment around him, the contemporary president sees that effort as worthwhile. He must deal with a Congress that is much more decentralized than the one his predecessors faced. No longer can powerful committee "barons" deliver votes, but the president must whip together his own coalitions. With a proliferation of interest groups in the nation over the past twenty years, the president finds that he cannot confine his interest-group politicking to a few major groups. The old New Deal "Grand Coalition" of labor and ethnic groups is not easily invoked to sway legislators. Consequently, "going public" makes sense because it offers the president a chance to move public opinion and thus move government.

But all this visibility makes the president vulnerable to shifts in public opinion or a poor television image. Jimmy Carter frequently used public politics, but it did not show him to best advantage. Indeed, as voters watched Carter look older each time he appeared on television, many believed him to be a failed president. High visibility is as risky as it is potentially useful.

With that fact in mind, Ronald Reagan came to office determined to make public politics work more effectively for him. To achieve that goal, he had to minimize the risks involved in a televised presidency. So, media access to Mr. Reagan was strictly controlled by him and his staff. He conducted public politics on his terms, leaving the media to live under his rules. Thus was born the paradox of the more visible but less accessible president.

PUBLIC POLITICS AND MEDIA COVERAGE

This paradox arises from the growing importance of television in national political life. Television is the primary source of political information for most Americans, the arena where political campaigns are fought, and the medium through which presidents can speak directly to voters.

Because television has assumed such importance to American politics, the images and information it conveys help to shape voters' impressions of the president, his subordinates and competitors, his policies, and the issues of the day. Therefore, it is not surprising that contemporary presidents tend to rely heavily on public politics to govern. The incumbent can literally appear in the nation's homes, not as a disembodied voice, but as a full-color image speaking directly to citizens. By so doing, he can bypass the "middleman" of television journalism and present his message exactly as he desires. Moreover, public politics has a logic unrelated to journalism: as Kernell has shown, it provides a way for presidents to pressure Congress to support the president's policies.

Presidents are prompted to "go public" because television makes it easier to do so and because television is not simply a "mirror" that reflects political reality. Rather, the structure of television journalism and behavior of journalists influence the images that appear in citizens' homes. Fred Smoller has examined the structure of television news coverage of the presidency, which he terms the "Six O'Clock Presidency," and demonstrated the non-neutral portrayal of the Chief Executive by the nation's primary news source.[2]

Smoller's analysis focuses on three factors in particular that influence the shape of the Six O'Clock Presidency: format constraint, the need for pictures, and assumptions about the nature of the viewing audience.[3] First, the format of television evening news, with less than a half hour per day, limits individual news reports generally to less than two minutes per item and requires that they be uncomplicated. The result, as Walter Cronkite has concluded, is "inadvertent and perhaps inevitable distortion."[4]

Second, television's need for pictures means that images are frequently used to present information. But they are flawed devices for doing so, because they oversimplify reality. Moreover, the need for pictures limits television coverage to actions (e.g., bill signings, protests outside the White House) rather than processes (e.g., the development of policy options, negotiations, etc.). Finally, it reinforces the journalistic tendency to focus on the unusual, such as a president tripping when leaving an airplane. These images may be interesting from a visual perspective, but they are often "gratuitous, trivial, and unrepresentative" of the realities of the presidency.[5]

Third, Smoller notes that television news executives assume that their viewers have a very limited attention span. In consequence, news reports rely on a "narrative form" that imparts an artificial shape to political developments and highlights conflict in the White House or between the president and his critics.[6]

The upshot for the president, according to Smoller, is that the Six O'Clock Presidency inherently tends to portray the president in a negative light. Therefore, presidents cannot assume that voters will receive a clear image of presidential policies and actions. What the voters receive is distorted in some way and this can damage the president's reputation. Beyond the Six O'Clock Presidency, the media are a force that can act to raise expectations in their coverage of extraordinary political events. Two events in recent political history serve as examples of this phenomenon. First, Ronald Reagan's selection of a vice-presidential running mate in 1980 was influenced by television. Before and during the Republican convention in Detroit, negotiations took place within high party circles to assemble a Ronald Reagan–Gerald Ford "dream ticket." Close television coverage of this story not only served to heighten expectations of such a deal among the public and many political leaders, but helped to prevent it as well. An on-camera interview between Gerald Ford and CBS correspondent Walter Cronkite fueled hopes that the "dream ticket" would arrive. But Mr. Ford's description of what Cronkite termed a "co-presidency" helped cast doubt in Ronald Reagan's mind about the prudence of such an arrangement. After all this speculation and an erroneous CBS News report that such a deal had been cut, the selection of George Bush seemed anticlimactic. As Jack Germond and Jules Witcover, two reporters covering the 1980 election, concluded about this affair:

Most notable about the episode was the effect of television. By broadcasting the hint that he might agree to go on the ticket, Ford moved the most important business of the 1980 Republican convention into public view. The resulting pressures in turn became a real factor in the deliberations.[7]

A second example was the 1986 summit meeting between President Reagan and Soviet Premier Mikhail Gorbachev in Reykjavik, Iceland. Television's coverage of the upcoming meeting put pressure on the president to reach an arms-control agreement with the Soviet Union. Once the summit was in progress, the presence of network news teams and their reports added to that pressure. As a result, the unsurprising (to expert observers) failure of the two leaders to reach an agreement stimulated much speculation about what went wrong and whether the president had been intransigent in negotiations.[8]

The president thus confronts the problem of media coverage that does not mirror reality: it distorts reality and sometimes influences it. These effects may even benefit a president, if they make his successes look grander (e.g., the Camp David accords or a major legislative success), but what is more likely is that they will not. So, post-modern presidents have an additional incentive to "go public." Their predecessors, notably Woodrow Wilson, used public politics to speak directly to voters over the heads of Congress and organized interests. Post-modern leaders "go public" to overrule the influence of these traditional adversaries, and now, the media.

For contemporary presidents, then, the mass media are both an ally and an adversary. How do they deal with it? The evidence suggests that they do so, and will continue to do so, by attempting to control "presidential news."

THE LOGIC OF IMAGE MANIPULATION

The president wants a favorable treatment by the media. Such treatment enables him to maintain or even improve his public standing, enhance his professional reputation, and assure himself that citizens are getting the correct message about administration policies and actions. But the Chief Executive will not receive this kind of coverage automatically, because of the problems discussed above. Indeed, all recent presidents and their press secretaries have lamented the failure of the news media to tell the true story or the whole story, at least as these actors have seen it.

What, then, do presidents do to correct this imbalance? They try to ensure that the president's perspective governs the reporting of "presidential news." Indeed, Ronald Reagan and his staff seemed to excel at this kind of approach. After examining the Reagan Administration's strategy for attacking this problem, Bruce Buchanan concludes that a new standard has been set for presidents who want not to be at the mercy of the media:

If press coverage is to help, not hurt, the president, control over access to information and the subject matter and content of presidential statements must be exercised by the administration, not the White House press corps.[9]

Buchanan sees the Reagan media strategy as a precedent for future presidents. Given the incentives for controlling "presidential news" described above, it is likely that future presidents will build on this precedent.

What was the Reagan strategy for controlling "presidential news": It was a set of coordinated approaches to news dissemination, actuated by the conviction that Mr. Reagan's message had to be conveyed to the nation whether the press corps liked it or not. First, public and media relations were the subject to much concern and active planning by senior presidential aides, particularly Deputy Chief of Staff Michael Deaver, Lawrence Barrett, a *Time* reporter who had access to some senior staff meetings during 1981, noted the consistent attention to public images among Mr. Reagan's aides:

... one concern permeated all those sessions: how events had played or would play on the air and in print. What items in the schedule should be turned into "photo ops?" Should the president have a question period with the press today? If he does, what story should be "sold?" Is the briefing material ready to prepare Reagan for his next magazine interview?... New inflation figures will come out this day; how should they best be described?... Later the visitor inquires whether this fare is typical of staff meeting agendas or whether some coincidence had bunched these items into a few sessions. Answers from three of the participants are unanimous: that was standard.[10]

The Reagan Administration was also the first to contain an Office of Communications that would coordinate the "message" flowing outward from the administration to the world: speechwriting, press relations, and all related activities. For both idiosyncratic and strategic reasons,[11] the White House Director of Communications came to supersede the Press Secretary in the administration's hierarchy of influence.

Second, the strategy held that relations between the White House and the press corps were to be conducted on the White House's terms, not reporters'. To that end, the president remained distant from the press corps. That meant a limited number of presidential press conferences, and the ones that did occur would follow specific rules. Ronald Reagan held fewer than thirty news conferences in his first term, compared with almost twice that number for Jimmy Carter.[12] What's more, a Reagan press conference was sedate by previous presidential standards. The president's staff made it clear at the beginning of the first term that Mr. Reagan would recognize only those reporters whose hands were raised, and would not respond to shouts of his name as his predecessors had done. Journalists were also required to remain seated when not actually called upon by the president, whereas previous press conferences had been conducted with reporters on their feet. The more controlled atmosphere of a Reagan press conference contributed to the appearance of a president in charge of his office. Reporters grumbled about the changes, but were forced to go along with them.

Outside of press conferences, the president's distance from reporters allowed him to ignore questions unless he wanted to respond. He chastened journalists for asking substantive questions at "photo opportunities," which were times reserved for photographing the president (and often some visitor). Upon leaving or arriving at the White House via helicopter, the president could choose to answer or ignore reporters' shouted questions as he saw fit. The wearer of a hearing aid, Mr. Reagan often pretended not to hear the press.

Third, the president's activities were planned with an eye to the visual impressions they would leave. Michael Deaver, sometimes called the "keeper of the presidential image," was sensitive to the subtle (or not-so-subtle) messages imparted by the visual setting for a presidential speech or announcement. As Deaver told the New York *Times*:

> Up until this president, you had housing starts going up and Jimmy Carter would go into the East room and announce the figures. We went out to Fort Worth, and in front of a scaffolding with carpenters working in the background Reagan says "housing starts are up." With 80% of the public getting its news from TV, the guy in the audience says to his wife "My Gold! They're building houses again."[13]

Many presidential appearances were planned with such an approach in mind. On the fortieth anniversary of D-Day, Mr. Reagan stood on the beach of Normandy with French President Francois Mitterand and spoke of defending freedom. The president spent a week in 1984 visiting national parks and other outdoor sites in order to underscore his record on the environment. Even the White House press room was given a kind of "stage," featuring a stately plaque bearing an image of the president's mansion, to lend a more dignified appearance to even the most routine announcements.

Finally, the president met informally with reporters for off-the-record discussions and questions. These meetings provided high-level "background" information for reporters and encouraged journalistic friendliness toward the president, but protected Mr. Reagan against damaging quotes or reporting of his misstatements.

In sum, the Reagan Administration had a coordinated strategy for dealing with the media. Critics branded it a type of image manipulation, but the logic behind such manipulation is not difficult to understand. Because of the non-neutral nature of television news coverage, the Reagan strategy helped to tip the balance of reporting in the president's favor. Even if the speech or appearance of the moment did not include a direct appeal to voters to support the president's policies, the very context and structure of presidential appearances on television became a form of public politics.

That strategy and its general success are what led Bruce Buchanan to regard the Reagan experience as a standard for future administrations. Future presidents will face a media environment similar to Mr. Reagan's whether or not they share his goals. Therefore, his successors are apt to attempt some degree of image manipulation, even if it is less than Mr. Reagan's.

But image manipulation also has it costs, not only for journalists but also for the public. It makes citizen evaluation of the president more difficult.

THE PROBLEM OF EVALUATION

The more visible but less accessible presidency presents a challenge for citizens seeking to judge a president's performance in office. They are called upon to evaluate him when they vote, when they respond to opinion polls, and when they compare his successors to him. But for citizens to do this effectively, they need information, and the televised rhetorical presidency is not designed to provide the information that voters need.

The American democratic republic requires that citizens choose and evaluate leaders. Evaluation once meant judgment of an incumbent seeking reelection or the memory of one officeholder affecting the choice of a new leader, but today evaluation is more current. Public opinion polls continually gauge support for a president and, when relevant, presidential candidates. So in recent years evaluation has taken on an immediacy that it did not have before.

How do citizens evaluate presidents? The evidence indicates that the public tends to focus on the achievements and outcomes that a president is able to deliver.[14] Conditions such as war, international crisis, and economic conditions account for fluctuations in presidential performance. In short, the public seems to want results: presidents who appear to be successful are rated highly, while those who appear to fail are regarded poorly.

To that extent, the president has an institutional interest in appearing to be successful. Because this success test influences voter's opinions, the president has much at stake in his appearance as a "winner" or "loser." Image manipulation thus becomes important to contemporary presidents, because a neutral attitude toward media coverage is likely to leave voters with negative impressions of the president. If he is to have a chance to look like a "winner," a post-modern president must actively work to protect himself.

The problem with these developments is that both voters and presidents are the victims of a sort of political injustice. Indeed, there is a kind of double bind to the whole situation. The president is evaluated on the basis of outcomes, but voters do not receive a neutral picture of presidential reality from television. So, the president takes measures to secure favorable media coverage, but in doing so interferes with effective public evaluation of his performance in office. Even without adopting the cynical view that no president wants accurate evaluations, only good evaluations, no one can say that the public interest is served by this situation.

What, then, can any one do to improve the quality of citizen evaluations? There are no easy answers. Many critics, even friendly ones, admonished Ronald Reagan to take a less aggressive approach to managing "presidential news," but to no avail. After all, the president and his advisors saw no change in the media to warrant such a change in administration policy. Bruce Buchanan and others have suggested civic education to improve voters' evaluation, but he admits that such a course is a long and difficult one.[15] Some critics of the media want to see a change in television's coverage of the president, but Smoller's work indicates that many of the problems a president faces are deeply rooted in the structure of television news.

Is there any hope? The answer is unclear. Civic education might help direct voters toward evaluative criteria other than success or failure, but its effects will be slow in coming. Moreover, civic education does nothing about the Six O'Clock Presidency. Television evening news programs still have the structure Smoller describes, but increasingly alternative sources of information are available for those who are interested. Political discussion programs, interviews, documentaries, and other formats all provide viewers with alternatives to the half-hour prepackaged news of the Six O'Clock Presidency, but the audience for these programs is small by television industry standards. Over time, it may be possible for civic educations and better information sources to move the president and the public away from the visibility/accessibility paradox.

90 Until such a change occurs, the post-modern presidency will continue to be marked by that paradox. Presidents want and need visibility to influence the direction of public policy, while the media want and need the president for news coverage. But the incumbent wants to control what voters receive as much as possible, because of his stake in the success test of citizen evaluations. Therefore, while current conditions prevail, presidential governance in the United States will filter through image manipulation and the Six O'Clock Presidency.

THE RHETORICAL PRESIDENCY AGAIN

Perhaps the problem lies even deeper than in the visibility/accessibility paradox. Perhaps it lies in the very nature of the rhetorical presidency.

Wilson's doctrine of the rhetorical presidency places the Chief Executive at the center of the political system. Indeed, it assumes that the system ought to be one of "presidential government": the president, as the nation's only nationally elected leader, is made the vessel for all expectations of governmental policy and performance. The consequence of such a role is a tremendous degree of responsibility, because citizens vest in the president their expectations for the whole system.

The doctrine of the rhetorical presidency has been the basis for the widespread view among students of the presidency that the office is inherently weak.[16] Indeed, Wilson himself held to that opinion. It has been the conventional wisdom among scholars for almost three decades.

How does the doctrine lead to that conclusion? It does so by noting the gap between expectations and power. With the president as the focus of national government, whether he operates by bargaining or public

politics, it's not surprising that voters apply a success test to the judgment of presidential performance. After all, he is the wearer of all those
hats and the bearer of the "glorious burden." But his power is not up
to the demands those roles imply. The political system, despite all
appearances to the contrary, is not merely one of presidential government. It is one of separated institutions sharing powers, with not only
Congress but also administrative and judicial bodies contending for
influence over public policy.

Yes, the view that the presidency is weak is correct, if one accepts
the notion that all expectations ought to be vested in that office. But
that notion is an unfair one, because it gives citizens a false impression
of their government and presidents an unrealistic set of expectations to
fulfill.

Does that mean that the presidency is doomed to failure? No, because
a number of factors help to keep the presidency working. First, while
the system is not strictly presidential government by nature, it does
respond to presidential leadership. A forceful president, whether it is
FDR, Kennedy, Johnson, or Reagan, can make an impact on the system
that is significant. Second, many of the changes described throughout
this book, in the revival of prerogative power or the control of the
Executive Branch, enable post-modern presidents to extend their powers
and sway the course of national affairs. Third, with the development
of image manipulation, the president is able to give the impression of
success. Since voter approval affects the president's ability to influence
Congress, that impression can be a big help. In sum, the presidency is
not doomed to failure because it is not as desperate as the conventional
wisdom holds it to be. It is not as strong as voters have come to expect,
but it is not as weak as many scholars fear.

But these developments do not let the televised rhetorical presidency
entirely off the hook. The public still holds high expectations and the
president strives to live up to them. So, it is likely that image manipulation and public politics will continue to be part of the presidency for
the foreseeable future. The former is a defense against the bad press
that can damage a president's public standing, while the latter is a tool
for moving government in the direction the president wants it to go.

The result is that the presidency in the eye of the beholder is something
of an artificial creature. What voters see on their televisions is something
constructed, whether by the media or the president, for public con-
sumption. That fact is the fundamental challenge that modern technology

presents to the American democratic republic: how to reconcile the system's need for citizen information with the structure of television news and presidential interests.

A RHETORICAL REPUBLIC?

How can that reconciliation be achieved? Perhaps the answer lies in the American system's prescription that "ambition must be made to counteract ambition."[17]

Despite the rhetorical presidency's assumption of presidential government, the American system has never become such a regime. Rather, Congress allowed itself to be eclipsed and for much of the period of the modern presidency permitted the illusion of presidential government to prevail. When the Vietnam War and Watergate shocked Congress out of that illusion, many of the changes described elsewhere in this book got under way.

The result was a resurgent Congress, a temporarily weakened presidency, and a shift of power to the bureaucracy. When presidential power was revived in more recent years, it could not again eclipse the legislature.

Congress had changed and its members were changing. They were becoming more adept at the same sort of media politics that presidents have mastered. In the 1980s, both chambers admitted television cameras and all non-secret congressional proceedings became accessible to the public. Overall, both congressional leaders and regular members were sharpening their skills at public politics. In doing so, they began preparing for competition with the rhetorical presidency for public support.

The rise of a more media-adept legislature seems a mixed kind of blessing. On the one hand, it holds forth the possibility that Congress can challenge the president in the forum of television, thus mitigating some of the problems of image manipulation. On the other hand, a rhetorical Congress raises the possibility that the distortions of television will only be exacerbated. Voters now have the opportunity to watch the give-and-take of executive–congressional relations in their homes, but what they see is distorted by the lens of television. Only a small portion of viewers trouble themselves to take the opportunity to watch the range of debates, discussions, and interviews available to supplement the Six O'Clock Presidency. Most viewers rely on the pre-packaged evening news for their information.

To that extent, citizen education becomes imperative. If voters are to be able to interpret and evaluate effectively the battles unfolding on their screens, they must be equipped with a sufficient knowledge of the political system and policy issues to make informed judgments.

The competition of president, Congress, and other bodies for public attention and support might induce these actors to promote civic education out of their own interest. For Congress to compete with the president, for example, members who challenge the Chief Executive must remind voters of Congress' legitimate role in national policymaking.

But public officials have a responsibility for civic education that extends beyond self-interest. In a democratic system, they are obliged to help voters understand the system because that is part of their job. Unfortunately, that part of the job has often been slighted. At the same time, scholars, journalists, and other public figures are obliged to join in the task of civic education, because that is part of their jobs as well.

Unfortunately, everyone wants someone else to do the job. Scholars provide a good example. In most universities around the country, the teaching of American government is frequently left to teaching assistants and part-time lecturers, or is performed perfunctorily by professors who cannot escape the task. Few senior scholars approach it with enthusiasm. When these scholars finally confront the veterans of such American politics courses as upperclassmen and graduate students, they then lament the students' poor understanding of the American system.

The combination of civic education and official responsibility could help alleviate these problems and overcome the challenges imposed by television. But there will be no quick fixed or easy solutions. Change will come slowly and, until it does, the visibility/accessibility paradox will prevail.

The American system will not collapse because of television, but that technology has permanently altered the practice of politics in this country. The presidency has adapted to these changes; the rest of the systems will have to do so as well.

NOTES

1. On the presidency and its paradoxes, see Cronin, *The State of the Presidency*, pp. 3–22.

2. Fred Smoller, "The six o'clock Presidency: Patterns of network news

coverage of the President," *Presidential Studies Quarterly* 16 (Winter 1986): 31–49.

3. Ibid.

4. Quoted in ibid., pp. 35–6.

5. Ibid., p. 37.

6. Ibid., p. 38.

7. Jack W. Germond and Jules Witcover, *Blue Smoke and Mirrors: How Reagan Won and Why Carter Lost the Election of 1980* (New York: Viking Press, 1981), pp. 181–4.

8. See the major newspapers and magazines of the period for a picture of the intense coverage. The major American television networks all had news crews and their anchors on the scene to focus public attention on the summit.

9. Bruce Buchanan, *The Citizen's Presidency* (Washington: Congressional Quarterly Press, 1987), p. 120.

10. Lawrence I. Barrett, *Gambling With History: Reagan in the White House* (New York: Penguin Books, 1983), p. 442.

11. President Reagan's Press Secretary, James Brady, was seriously wounded in the attempt on Mr. Reagan's life in 1981. Brady kept his post and continued to serve as a sort of consultant to the administration, but the Office of Communications took over for day-to-day management of press relations.

12. Buchanan, p. 121.

13. New York *Times*, June 13, 1985, p. 14.

14. See Buchanan, op. cit.; Barilleaux, *The President and Foreign Affairs*, p. 50; Charles W. Ostrom, Jr., and Dennis M. Simon, "The President and public support: A strategic perspective," in *The Presidency and Public Policy Making*, pp. 50–70; idem., "Promise and performance: A dynamic model of Presidential popularity," *American Political Science Review* 79 (June 1985): 334–358; and Paul A. Anderson, "Deciding how to decide in foreign affairs: Decision-making strategies as solutions to Presidential problems," in *The Presidency and Public Policy Making*, pp. 151–172.

15. Buchanan, p. 201.

16. This view receives its clearest expression in Neustadt.

17. James Madison, *The Federalist*, No. 51.

7

Post-Modern Politics in the United States

American politics have undergone a number of dramatic changes in the past half-century, such that it is not precisely the same system that Franklin Roosevelt or even John Kennedy knew. It has been marked by war, depression, riots, social and economic change, technology, and time.

The last two decades have been an era of "newness" in the nation's politics. There is the "new Congress" that developed after 1974; the "new American political system" discerned in 1978; the rise of the "New Right" after the decline of the "New Left"; and the recent turn to the "new direction in American politics." What of the presidency, which has been at the center of American politics at least since the 1930s? Is it also new?

If the argument of this book is correct, then the nation possesses not so much a new presidency as a "revised edition" of the office. The contemporary, post-modern presidency is the third "edition" of the role created for George Washington. It has not remained unscathed by the changes of recent decades.

IS THE PRESIDENCY REALLY THAT DIFFERENT?

The basic issue that this book has tackled is the question of difference. Yes, critics will reply, these changes in presidential style or White

House management are significant and real, but they do not indicate a change in the office. After all, has the role of the presidency in the political system been altered? The answer is a guarded "yes."

The Post-Modern Presidency Is Different

The post-modern presidency is different from the modern presidency in two essential ways: 1) its role in the larger political order is somewhat different from that of the previous "edition"; and, more significantly, 2) the ways in which post-modern presidents fulfill the president's role in the system have changed.

The role of the presidency in the political system is not exactly the same today as it was in the heyday of the modern presidency. That statement is true because the political system has changed. Where the modern presidency existed in a system dominated by the vicissitudes of presidential–congressional relations, the contemporary system features significant policymaking power in regulatory and judicial bodies. Regardless of how the Chief Executive and the two chambers on Capitol Hill are getting along, these alternative centers of policymaking continue to function. To that extent, both the presidency and Congress have seen their roles altered.

Beyond that development, the role of the presidency has been altered by the changing political agenda. The modern presidency was closely associated with the liberal agenda; but its post-modern successor is not exactly linked with any agenda. Ronald Reagan made the office into an instrument of conservative action, which confused those observers who assumed that presidential activism could only serve expansionist goals. Mr. Reagan's successors will probably employ their powers to different ends, but there is no longer a necessary connection between the office and specific policy goals.

These changes make the post-modern presidency distinct from earlier "editions" of the office. The Oval Office is now one of several power centers in Washington and an institution for promoting a wider variety of ends. Of course, future presidents will continue to promote the interests of the office they inhabit, and will not be merely "one of the crowd" in the Washington community, but they will have a somewhat different role in American politics than their predecessors.

More important than role modification, however, is the fact of changes in the ways the presidency operates. Most of this book has examined the revisions in presidential power, prerogatives, management, tools for influence, and methods of operation, and these developments are the major reasons for the post-modern presidency. As noted above, the contemporary office is more a revised "edition" than a complete rewriting of what existed before, and it is so because of these changes in the way presidents perform their role.

The trend toward "going public," the development of a more "complete" presidency through changing prerogatives, the growing importance of presidential appointments, the growing complexity of presidential management, and the more exacting skills required for dealing with a new Congress, all combine to alter significantly the way that a president fulfills his role in the political order. These changes distinguish the conduct of the contemporary presidency from the life of earlier editions.

So What?

These changes in the presidency are significant, not merely because of some pedantic distinctions between the previous and current "editions" of the office, but because they affect several aspects of the institution that any observer would accept as important: presidential relations with Congress, the skills needed by presidents, the evaluation of national politics in the late twentieth century. As the following analysis will demonstrate, the fact of the post-modern presidency has implications for all facets of America's single most important office. To that extent, the rise of the post-modern presidency also has implications for the future of presidency studies. Each of these issues will be examined in this chapter.

THE POST-MODERN PRESIDENCY MEETS THE NEW CONGRESS

To a greater extent than in any other political system, the American republic is governed by a number of relationships. Tripartite government in the United States makes relations between the branches profoundly important to what the government does or does not do. As a result, public policy is framed as much by interbranch relations as by public opinion, political culture and ideology, partisanship, or any other factor.

Foremost in this system is the relationship between the president and

Congress. That relationship is not the same as the relationship of only two decades past, but has changed in a number of ways.

How are post-modern executive–congressional relations different from what came before? Structurally, they differ in that the president must now act as "chief whip" in the legislature if he is to win support for his proposals. Moreover, relations between the branches have become much more public, with television as the arena in which conflicts between the president and Congress are often played out. Not only have recent presidents tended to use politics more frequently than did their predecessors, but members of Congress are now more adept at using electronic media to compete with the Chief Executive.

In terms of issues, two features distinguish contemporary executive–congressional relations from those of the past. One is the prominence, if not dominance, of budgetary issues. With the budget used more and more frequently as the central instrument for governing the nation, the congressional budget cycle has come to set the pace for interbranch interactions. Moreover, congressional budget making in recent years has tended to involve omnibus budget bills rather than a string of individual appropriations, so the budget process invites debate over the entire realm of national policy. The budget thus serves as the battleground on which substantive policy issues are fought—from strategic defense to healthcare reforms—so conflicts between the president and Congress will center around that document and the policy consequences of appropriations. That fact, plus continuing fiscal stress as a characteristic of the national economic scene, means that budgetary issues will continue to dominate national politics for the foreseeable future.

Second, foreign policy conflict has become a fixture of recent American politics. With the breakdown of the postwar foreign-policy consensus during the Vietnam War, the United States moved into a period of conflict over its relations with the rest of the world. Members of Congress are active participants in that conflict and not willing to allow the president to dominate American international relations without criticism. Republicans and Democrats, liberals and conservatives, all have demonstrated a greater willingness to challenge the president on foreign affairs than did their predecessors in the years from the 1940s through the early 1960s.

Because of that willingness, presidents will likely look to their prerogative powers for the means to conduct foreign policy with minimal interruption from Congress. The recent revival of presidential prerogative power in foreign policy was stimulated by a presidential determination to circumvent the constraints imposed by Congress during the "congressional revolution" of the mid–1970s. In the post-modern era, that determination is likely to remain, because presidents will continue to try to avoid limits on their powers. Since appropriations provide an important means by which Congress can check the president, legislators will continue to use (or try to use) Congress' power of the purse to restrain presidential autonomy. The result of these competing developments will be more presidential use of prerogatives in order to avoid frequent congressional attempts to influence policy through the budget.

Taken together, these developments will reinforce the centrality of the budget in national policymaking. Indeed, the post-modern era is likely to be the "age of the budget," because so much of governing will be conducted through that instrument. Policy disputes will be manifest in budgetary disputes.

Where will these budgetary disputes lead? The answer is not certain, but could be grim. Continued battles over the budget, if unchecked, could mean an extension of the budgetary politics of recent years: a politics of big deficits because of disagreement between the branches over spending priorities, tax levels, and the distribution of sacrifice. Unable to come to terms over the budget, the two political branches might maintain the large gap between taxes and spending. A different president or a change in congressional leadership will not guarantee the end to budgetary disagreements. Rather, because of the centrality of the budget and competition between the executive and the legislature, these disputes are likely to continue. There is no consensus among economists about the ultimate effect of long-term deficits, but few suggest that it would be healthy for the economy.

Some critics have tried to pin the blame for recent large deficits on Ronald Reagan, "big spenders" in Congress, or elsewhere, but these explanations assume that a balanced budget is a simple matter of political will. Rather than a matter of will, it may be that big deficits are the consequence of a structural phenomenon in American politics: that conflict between the president and Congress exacerbates the tendency of democratic politics to tax low and spend high.[1] Because there is disagreement over spending priorities, plus political pressure to maintain high levels of government services along with low levels of taxation, resolution of the nation's deficit problems is unlikely at any time in the near future.

Ultimately, the result of continued large deficits may be the imposition of limits on deficit spending, such as through a constitutional amendment to require a balanced budget. Short of such strictures, or a miraculous consensus on just how to balance the budget, political leaders can dream of "growing out" of the deficit through economic expansion.

Whatever happens to the deficit, it and overall budgetary issues will be the most prominent concerns for executive-congressional relations in the near future. Presidents will try to use their increased leverage over executive budget making, public politics, and legislative liaison agents to whip together coalitions in support of their budgets. Congress, however, will resist those efforts, unless a popular president can bring public pressure to bear on the legislature.

The result of these developments will be a demand on future presidents to exhibit skills that their predecessors were not required to have. Post-modern presidents need skills suited for an age of budgeting and regulation.

POST-MODERN PRESIDENTIAL SKILLS

Exactly what kinds of skills are required of post-modern presidents? Three general types are involved: political, legislative, and managerial.

Political Skills

Post-modern presidents need two particular political skills. One is the ability to think strategically. This ability has always been required of presidents in some degree, but in contemporary politics it is needed more than ever. Why? Because there is essentially no time for a president to learn from his mistakes. The pace of the presidency has increased considerably in recent years.

Lyndon Johnson was known to observe that a president had only one year to accomplish anything, because afterward he would be bogged down in congressional or presidential electoral politics. Since his time, the period of one year seems a luxury for a new president. Because the Chief Executive must take charge of the presidential establishment and put his own house in order before he can do much else, he must think strategically about making his administration work.

Paul Light has warned that contemporary incumbents face the prospects of a "no-win" presidency,[2] because of cross-pressures from competing political interests, presidential goals, and inexperience early in an administration. In the terms discussed here, presidents face the prospect that they will accomplish little because the new political environment makes effective presidential action more difficult: interest group proliferation, a new political agenda, fiscal stress, the "new" Congress, the Six O'Clock Presidency, and other factors all stand in the way of the president.

If the new incumbent is to deal with these problems and have any chance of overcoming them, he must think strategically about how to proceed. Strategic presidential thinking begins with good organization and staffing, and is followed by a sense of priorities about what he intends to accomplish, a media strategy, and a sense of direction.

In short, contemporary presidents need more than a legislative agenda if they are to succeed. Strategic thinking means a more comprehensive view of the office and the president's responsibilities and powers. It especially involves a sense of how the president's general secretariat will help him to get where he wants to go, and how the president will relate to his staff.

In addition, post-modern presidents need the capacity to use public politics. Because the new political environment encourages incumbents to do so, potential officeholders need the skills necessary to survive in politics in the media age. In this regard, upon losing the 1984 presidential election, Walter Mondale commented, "Modern politics requires a mastery of television. I've never really warmed up to television and, in fairness to television, it's never warmed up to me."[3] Mondale's political style was one of a pre-television age, which hampered his bid for the presidency in the post-modern age.

But this need for skill at public politics goes beyond campaigning. As the trend of "going public" makes clear, presidents in office rely on his kind of politics. So, incumbents must be able to function effectively on television and employ a media strategy for making the best of the intense coverage a president receives. Without such skills and such a strategy, the Chief Executive will lack a lever for moving Congress and be more vulnerable to the problems of the Six O'Clock Presidency.

Legislative Skills

Post-modern presidents also need legislative skills, but in a way that is different from their predecessors. First, contemporary officeholders need a clear sense of budgetary priorities, because it is in the budget process that many of the most important substantive decisions of national policy are made. If a new president is going to make his mark on national policy, his strategy for affecting government must include budgeting.

For that reason, among others, future presidents will likely maintain the system of top-down budgeting imposed in recent years. Without such an approach to executive budget construction, the Chief Executive risks losing the initiative in policy to Congress or the bureaucracy. By employing a system of top-down budgeting, the president can increase his leverage in the struggle to shape national policy.

To see that budget, as well as other proposals, passed into law in some form he considers acceptable, the president must also possess the kinds of skills associated with a legislative whip. As Chapter 1 demonstrated, he must be able to "work" the Congress as a whip does, in order to assemble coalitions in support of his proposals: meet with members, make phone calls, maintain good relations with legislative leaders, stay abreast of changing legislative alignments and personnel, engage in public and private politicking, and generally work harder than his predecessors did.

The key to success as "chief whip" in Congress is an effective legislative liaison staff. The staff will be the president's arms and legs in his quest for legislative success. He must not only appoint it, but, as with all of his other subordinates, carefully manage these legislative aides in order to accomplish his goals in the "new" Congress.

This increased legislative workload makes the president's job all the more demanding, so the Chief Executive must excel in one final category of skills: management. The post-modern president must be a far more effective manager than those who preceded him in the Oval Office.

Management Skills

What distinguishes contemporary presidential management from the operations of earlier "editions" of the office is the need for the president to be able to work at the head of a large, complex, and somewhat established bureaucracy. This need runs counter to much of the conventional wisdom on White House management.

Much of conventional thought on presidential management, fondly remembering FDR and JFK, tends to regard the White House in terms of small group dynamics and organizational fluidity. The conventional wisdom has long been that the president ought to be his own chief of staff, delegate little, and keep all subordinates at peak performance by close management of the administration.

The reality of the contemporary presidency is quite different from that view. It's not that a president must now be a competent administration, because he has long needed to be just that, but that the Chief Executive must be able to work through others. He must be able to delegate power to his senior aides, function in an environment of relatively fixed staff structures (e.g., OMB, NSC), employ a chief of staff to hold the general secretariat together, maintain a continuous search for talented aides and appointees, and balance delegation with his own responsibility and obligations in office. If a president cannot really act through others, he cannot really function as president. As the discussion throughout this book has made clear, contemporary presidents are pulled in many directions. They must do all that was expected of their predecessors, plus work harder on Congress, public politics, and White House management. Without the ability to preside as well as to propose and persuade, the Chief Executive will be overwhelmed.

Does that mean that the presidency has become an impossible job? The answer depends on one's perspective. If one expects the president to "go it along," channel everything into the Oval Office, lead, inspire, and command, then no one is up to that job. But if one accepts the need for and the legitimacy of a president seeking help from his senior aides, then the tasks involved in the job are merely herculean and not impossible. The presidency will never be an easy position, but it can be made all the harder by the notion that the Chief Executive cannot delegate.

What this means for prospective presidents is that they must acquire the management skills necessary for office before coming to office. Experience certainly helps to build these skills or to identify them, but just any experience with administration will not do. Rather, a contender for the presidency ought to be able to demonstrate, at least to his own satisfaction, an ability to work with a large political bureaucracy while other responsibilities compete for the individual's time.

What's more, if they intend to succeed, prospective presidents must abandon any hope of surrounding themselves with a cadre of loyalists who have limited experience but are devoted to the boss. Such aides have a place, but running the White House requires the kind of competence and experience not often developed in the shadow of a single politician. If the future president can think in terms of his institutional needs rather than surrounding himself with loyalists, he will have a better chance of achieving his goals.

All of this is not to say that a president ought not expect loyalty from his aides. Of course he should, buy loyalty alone will not do the job he needs done. The president needs help that is constructive. One way to ensure that he gets such help is to abide by the Rule of Defensibility: choose senior aides as if their appointments required Senate confirmation. Such an approach, plus its corollary that everything done in the White House must be defensible before Congress, would at least allow the president to construct an inner circle that would enhance his chances of success.

So, the post-modern president must be more skilled at management than his predecessors. He must also give it more attention, lest he lose control of his own domain. Without getting his own house in order, the Chief Executive will succumb to the fate of Light's "no win" presidency.

CHOOSING AND JUDGING POST-MODERN PRESIDENTS

If post-modern presidents are to possess these skills and perform as the contemporary office demands, then the process of choosing candidates and judging presidents ought to reflect such needs. As it exists, however, the process for choice and judgment does not perform as expected. It is not completely inappropriate for the tasks involved, but neither is it ideally suited for its work.

The contemporary presidential selection process, being entrepreneurial in nature, does favor those candidates who can mount a long-term strategy for building support in a complex and ambiguous nomination and election system. To survive in that system, candidates must build and operate large staffs that can deal with all aspects of modern campaigning. To that extent, the process demands of candidates some of the skills that post-modern presidents need: the ability to build and manage a large staff, the ability to use public politics, the ability to think strategically, and the ability to deal with frustration and ambiguity. Despite criticisms that it is too long, complex, and expensive, the current system does not do a bad job of testing certain necessary presidential skills.

What the system does not test, however, are legislative skills and the full range of presidential management skills. Nor do journalists reporting on presidential candidates really focus sufficiently on these matters. The current system has no provision for assessing a potential president's capacity for acting as "chief whip" in Congress.

Management is also slighted. The system does require a candidate to build a large operation to help him win election, but managing a campaign is different from managing the White House. A good example of this point was Hamilton Jordan, Jimmy Carter's top aide and later his chief of staff. Jordan was a skillful campaign manager, but ran into a number of problems because of his inexperience at governmental management, and even once lamented that there was no place for campaign managers such as himself to go between elections. A candidate's ability to manage his won campaign does not fully indicate his ability to manage in the Oval Office.

Because of these problems, the selection process needs ways to test or reveal candidate abilities in legislative coalition building and governmental management. Experience, of course, is the best indicator in these areas, so a greater focus on candidate experience is needed. Contemporary journalism tends to focus on three aspects of a candidate: his public image and personality, his highly nuanced positions on issues, and his place in the horse race that is the campaign (delegate count, strategy, stand in the polls, etc.). It does not give much attention to a candidate's qualifications and preparations for office, at least as they apply to his ability to function in office. Candidates, of course, do not care to focus on such issues, unless they believe that these factors will help them win. So they seldom do, because voters do not seem to pay much attention to these things either.

On the other hand, perhaps if voters were supplied with more information on these topics, and led to understand their importance, then citizen attention to candidates might focus on these matters. For whatever reason, the current system is deficient in this regard.

The evaluation of presidents is also deficient, because it focuses on outcomes and appearances. Voters, commentators, and even scholars tend to view presidential performance in terms of the results achieved, and to assume that success or failure is the result of good processes in policymaking.[4] In other words, presidential observers do not really look at presidential skills and management in themselves, but tend to connect them to the results they perceive flowing from a president's performance. This sort of evaluation does an injustice to incumbents and to citizens, because it does not assess presidential performance so much as it assesses the conditions during a president's term.

In the post-modern era, however, evaluation must be more sophisticated. If citizens and professional president watchers are to make more informed evaluations of incumbents and candidates, they need information about the range of candidate qualifications and incumbent performances. They also need a better understanding of what kinds of responsibilities and powers are involved in the contemporary presidency. This book is an effort to facilitate a better understanding of the presidency in the late twentieth century.

FUTURE STUDY OF THE PRESIDENCY

The post-modern presidency, as it has been surveyed in this book, implies new directions for research on this political institution. Because the office has changed, presidency studies ought to reflect the changes involved.

First, there ought to be renewed attention to the subject of presidential management. The 1986 conference of former presidential aides, along with the fiftieth anniversary of the Brownlow Committee's report and the developments reported on here, all point to the need for new research into the issues of the administrative presidency.

These issues include the organization and management of the White House staff in this age of a presidential "general secretariat," the relationship between the presidency and the bureaucracy (in the wake of administrative clearance and other developments), the presidency's role in a system of government characterized by regulation and administration, the character and operations of OMB and its role in the Executive Branch, the relationship between the White House staff and Congress (especially in light of the Iran-Contra affair); and the institutionalization of the White House chief of staff.

Second, the increasing presidential use of public politics, image manipulation, and related developments, point to the need for more attention to the public presidency. These developments not only imply the need for research into presidential efforts at gaining public support, but also the effects of such efforts on the political system. As Congress and other political actors cultivate their abilities to use public politics and the media, American democracy will be altered. Scholars are only beginning to examine the consequences of these phenomena.

The foregoing comments point to a third area of concern: presidential evaluation. The thrust of this book has been to report on and suggest the consequences of the rise of the post-modern presidency. That new "edition" of the office requires a new understanding of presidential assessment. As comments throughout this work have suggested, president watchers must pay closer attention to how the office has changed, in its powers, behavior, means of acting, goals, and other aspects. So, presidential evaluation must be brought up to date, to consider what must be done if the Chief Executive's performance is to be accurately assessed. And to consider how presidents are chosen.

Therefore, the study of the presidency needs a focus on the future of the office. It is not so much that scholars and other observers of the presidential institution are looking for the wrong things, but that they need a better focus on how the office has changed in the recent past and what those changes will mean in the future.

NOTES

1. For thoughts on this subject, see Daniel Patrick Moynihan, "The 'new science of politics' and the old art of government," *The Public Interest* 86(Winter 1987): 22–35; and, James Q. Wilson, "Does the separation of powers still work?" *The Public Interest* 86(Winter 1987): 36–52.

2. Light, *The President's Agenda*, pp. 202–3.

3. New York *Times*, November 8, 1984, p. 17.

4. See Barilleaux, *The President and Foreign Affairs*, pp. 158–77.

Epilogue

Because the presidency is occupied by an individual, the office and the officeholder are often confused. Judgments of the institution, its powers and functions, frequently are tied up in reactions to the incumbent of the day or a hero or villain of the recent past. For years, presidents lived in the shadow of Franklin Roosevelt or John Kennedy. Today, they live with the shade of Richard Nixon. Tomorrow, for better or worse, they will live with the legacy of Ronald Reagan.

If only by virtue of being the first two-term president in twenty years, Mr. Reagan has influenced the shape of the contemporary presidency. But, more significantly, because of his distinctive agenda, attitudes, popularity, and style, he has left a mark on his office that will affect future incumbents.

But the presidency of the late twentieth century, which I characterize as the post-modern presidency, is more than a creature of Mr. Reagan. It is the result of trends that began at least twenty years ago—and some are even older—that were consolidated in the past years. The rise of the post-modern presidency was not inevitable, but had Mr. Reagan never assumed office revisions in the office would still have occurred. What he did was to accelerate the process and give it the particular shape it has acquired.

Presidents in the late twentieth century, then, will be post-modern presidents. They will attempt to govern through a mix of prerogative power, public politics, and old-fashioned bargaining. They will focus much of their attention on budgeting and regulation, because they will live in a governing system that operates through those devices. But their appointments, whether consciously or no, will also contribute to each incumbent's ultimate impact on the nation.

Post-modern presidents will need to be better managers than their predecessors. Whereas the modern presidency of midcentury was thought to be a position of legislative leadership requiring a master lawmaker, the contemporary office is more a position of administration and management. For that reason, as well as changes in the nominating system, governors and other executives once again make good candidates for the nation's highest office.

Indeed, changes in the presidency and national policy have revived the American governorship in a way once considered impossible. In the era of federal government expansion, governors were left behind as power flowed to Washington. In the 1970s and 1980s, however, as fiscal stress occurred throughout the nation, executive leadership in the states once again became a valuable commodity. That fact, plus the development of an entrepreneurial nominating system that favored "outsiders," revived the governorship as a stepping-stone to the White House.

Whoever steps into the Oval Office in these late-century decades will need to be skilled at running a large bureaucracy—no, not the Executive Branch, but the Executive Office of the President—and so will need extensive management skills. The first order of business for any future incumbents, regardless of their policy goals, will be to set his or her own house in order.

Unless the president does so, he will be overwhelmed by a governing system and a political environment that has many centers of power: in a fragmented Congress, in the courts and regulatory agencies, in the executive bureaucracy, in a profusion of interest groups, in the media, in the states, and finally, in the White House. This environment of diffused power is open to influence by a president, buy only one knows the rules and how to play the game.

This book has attempted to give a picture of both the rules and the game, in order to guide future presidents, students of the presidency, and perplexed citizens. The American political system was designed to be complex, but also comprehensible, and this work will serve its purpose if it makes some sense out of new twists in that part of the system called the presidency.

Bibliography

Abraham, Henry J. *Justices and Presidents*. New York: Penguin Books, 1974.

Agresto, John. *The Supreme Court and Constitutional Democracy*. Ithaca, NY: Cornell University Press, 1984.

Anderson, Patrick. *The President's Men*. Garden City, NY: Doubleday, 1969.

Anderson, Paul A. "Deciding how to decide in foreign affairs: Decision-making strategies as solutions to presidential problems." In *The Presidency and Public Policy Making*, pp. 151–172. Edited by George C. Edwards III, Steven Shull, and Norman Thomas. Pittsburgh: University of Pittsburgh Press, 1985.

Argyle, Nolan J., and Ryan J. Barilleaux. "Past failures and future prescriptions for presidential management reform." *Presidential Studies Quarterly* 16 (Fall 1986): 716–733.

Ball, Howard. *Controlling Regulatory Sprawl*. Westport, CT: Greenwood Press, 1984.

Barber, James David. *The Presidential Character*, 3rd ed. Englewood Cliffs, NJ: Prentice-Hall, 1985.

Barger, Harold M. *The Impossible Presidency: Illusions and Realities of Executive Power*. Glenview, IL: Scott-Foresman, 1984.

Barilleaux, Ryan J. "Aide's-eye view of the Senate." *Christian Science Monitor*, May 15, 1978, p. 21.

———. "Executive non-agreements, arms control, and the invitation to struggle in foreign affairs." *World Affairs* 148 (Fall 1986): 217–28.

———. "Kennedy, the Bay of Pigs, and the limits of collegial decisionmaking." In *The Presidency and National Security Policy*, pp. 207–22. Edited by R. Gordon Hoxie. New York: Center for the Study of the Presidency, 1984.

————. "Parallel unilateral policy declarations: A new device for presidential autonomy in foreign affairs." *Presidential Studies Quarterly* 17 (Winter 1987): 107–117.

————. *The President and Foreign Affairs: Evaluation, performance, and Power*. New York: Praeger, 1985.

Barrett, Laurence I. *Gambling With History: Reagan in the White House*. New York: Penguin Books, 1984.

Beer, Samuel. "In search of a new public philosophy." In *The New American Political System*, pp. 5–44. Edited by Anthony King. Washington: American Enterprise Institute, 1978.

Berger, Raoul. *Government by Judiciary*. Cambridge, MA: Harvard University Press, 1977.

Berman, Larry. *The Office of Management and Budget and the Presidency, 1921–1979*. Princeton: Princeton University Press, 1979.

Bernstein, Carl, and Bob Woodward. *All the President's Men*. New York: Simon and Schuster, 1974.

Bonafede, Dom. "The new model year." *National Journal* (November 26, 1977): 1859.

Brown, Lawrence D. *New Policies, New Politics: Government's Response to Government's Growth*. Washington: Brookings Institution, 1983.

Brzezinski, Zbigniew. *Power and Principle*. New York: Farrar, Strauss, and Giroux, 1983.

Buchanan, Bruce. *The Citizen's Presidency*. Washington: Congressional Quarterly Press, 1987.

Cannon, Lou. *Reagan*. New York: Putnam, 1982.

Caro, Robert A. *The Years of Lyndon Johnson, Volume I: The Path to Power*. New York: Vintage Books, 1981.

Ceasar, James. *Reforming the Reforms*. Washington: Ballinger; 1982.

————. *Presidential Selection*. Princeton: Princeton University Press, 1979.

————. "The rhetorical presidency revisited." *Modern Presidents and the Presidency*, pp. 15–34. Edited by Marc Landy. Lexington, MA: Lexington Books, 1985.

————, Glenn Thurow, Jeffrey Tulis, and Joseph Bessette. "The rise of the rhetorical presidency." *Presidential Studies Quarterly* 11 (Spring 1981): 233–251.

Chubb, John E., and Paul E. Peterson (eds.). *The New Direction in American Politics*. Washington: The Brookings Institution, 1985.

————. "Realignment and institutionalization." In *The New Direction in American Politics*, pp. 1–32. Edited by John E. Chubb and Paul E. Peterson. Washington: Brookings Institution, 1985.

Cronin, Thomas E. "Rethinking the vice-presidency." In *Rethinking the Presidency*, pp. 324–48. Edited by Thomas E. Cronin. Boston: Little, Brown, 1982.

————. *The State of the Presidency*, 2nd ed. Boston: Little, Brown, 1980.

————. "The swelling of the presidency." *Saturday Review* 1 (February 1973): 30–36.

Crotty, William, and John S. Jackson III. *Presidential Primaries and Nominations*. Washington: Congressional Quarterly Press, 1985.

Cutler, Lloyd. "To form a government—on the defects of separation of powers." *Foreign Affairs* 59 (Fall 1980): 126–43.

Daly, John Charles, et al. *President vs. Congress: Does the Separation of Powers Still Work?* AEI Forum 47. Washington: American Enterprise Institute, 1981.

Davis, Eric L. "Congressional liaison: The people and the institutions." In *Both Ends of the Avenue*, pp. 59–95. Edited by Anthony King. Washington: Enterprise Institute, 1983.

Destler, I. M. "National security II: The rise of the assistant (1961–1981)." In *The Illusion of Presidential Government*, pp. 263–85. Edited by Hugh Heclo and Lester M. Salamon. Boulder, CO: Westview Press, 1981.

Draper, Theodore. "Reagan's junta." *New York Review of Books*, January 29, 1987, pp. 5–14.

Edward, George C., III. *Presidential Influence in Congress*. San Francisco: W.H. Freeman, 1980.

————. *The Public President*. New York: St. Martin's Press, 1983.

Evans, Rowland, and Robert Novak. *Lyndon B. Johnson: The Exercise of Power*. New York: New American Library, 1966.

Fenno, Richard F. "The House Appropriations Committee as a political system: The problem of integration." In *Studies of Congress*, pp. 199–221. Edited by Glenn R. Parker. Washington: Congressional Quarterly Press, 1985.

Fisher, Louis. *Constitutional Conflicts Between Congress and the Presidency*. Princeton: Princeton University Press, 1985.

Flaumenhauft, Harvey. "Hamilton's administrative republic and the American presidency." In *The Presidency in the Constitutional Order*, pp. 65–112. Edited by Joseph M. Bessette and Jeffrey Tulis. Baton Rouge: Louisiana State University Press, 1981.

Franck, Thomas, and Edward Weisband. *Foreign Policy by Congress*. New York: Oxford University Press, 1979.

Franklin, Daniel Paul. "War powers in the modern context." *Armed Forces and Society* (forthcoming).

————. "Why the legislative veto isn't dead." *Presidential Studies Quarterly* 16 (Summer 1986): 491–502.

George, Alexander L. *Presidential Decisionmaking in Foreign Policy: The Effective Use of Information and Advice*. Boulder, CO: Westview Press, 1980.

―――, and Juliette L. George. *Woodrow Wilson and Colonel House*. New York: J. Day and Co., 1956.

Germond, Jack W., and Jules Witcover. *Blue Smoke and Mirrors: How Reagan Won and Why Carter Lost the Election of 1980*. New York: Viking Press, 1981.

Goldman, Peter, and Tony Fuller, et al. *The Quest for the Presidency 1984*. New York: Bantam Books, 1985.

Goldstein, J. K. *The Modern American Vice Presidency*. Princeton: Princeton University Press, 1982.

Graber, Doris A. *Mass Media and American Politics*. Washington: Congressional Quarterly Press, 1980.

Graham, Otis L., Jr. *Toward a Planned Society*. New York: Oxford University Press, 1976.

Grant, Ruth Weissboard, and Stephen Grant. "The Madisonian presidency." In *The Presidency in the Constitutional Order*, pp. 31–64. Edited by Joseph M. Bessette and Jeffrey Tulis. Baton Rouge: Louisiana State University Press, 1981.

Greenstein, Fred I. "Change and continuity in the modern presidency." *The New American Political System*, pp. 45–86. Edited by Anthony King. Washington: American Enterprise Institute, 1978.

―――, editor. *The Reagan Presidency: An Early Assessment*. Baltimore: Johns Hopkins University Press, 1982.

―――, Larry Berman, and Alvin S. Felzenberg, with Doris Lidtke. *Evolution of the Modern Presidency: A Bibliographic Survey*. Washington: American Enterprise Institute, 1977.

Hamilton, Alexander, James Madison, and John Jay. *The Federalist Papers*, with an introduction by Clinton Rossiter. New York: New American Library, 1961.

Hargrove, Edwin, and Michael Nelson. *Presidents, Politics, and Policy*. Baltimore: Johns Hopkins University Press, 1984.

Heclo, Hugh. "Executive budget making." *Federal Budget Policy in the 1980s*, pp. 261–290. Edited by Gregory B. Mills and John Palmer. Washington: Urban Institute Press, 1984.

―――. "OMB and the Presidency—The problem of neutral competence." In *Bureaucratic Power in National Policy Making*, 4th ed., pp. 106–19. Edited by Francis Rourke. Boston: Little, Brown, 1986.

―――, and Rudolph G. Penner. "Fiscal and political strategy in the Reagan administration." In *The Reagan Presidency: An Early Assessment*, pp. 21–47. Edited by Fred I. Greenstein. Baltimore: Johns Hopkins University Press, 1982.

Henderson, Phillip G. "Advice and decision: The Eisenhower National Security Policy reappraised." In *The Presidency and National Security Policy*, pp. 153–86. Edited by R. Gordon Hoxie. New York: Center for the Study of the Presidency, 1984.

Hess, Stephen. *Organizing the Presidency*. Washington: The Brookings Institution, 1976.

Hodgson, Godfrey. *All Things to All Men: The False Promise of the Modern American Presidency*. New York: Simon and Schuster, 1980.

Holtzman, Abraham. *Legislative Liaison: Executive Leadership in Congress*. Chicago: Rand McNally, 1970.

Hoxie, R. Gordon. *Command Decision and the Presidency*. New York: Reader's Digest Press, 1977.

Hunter, Robert. *Presidential Control of Foreign Policy*. The Washington Papers, No. 91. New York: Praeger and the Center for Strategic and International Studies, Georgetown University, 1982.

Janis, Irving. *Victims of Groupthink*. Boston: Houghton Mifflin, 1972.

Johnson, Loch K. *The Making of International Agreements: Congress Confronts the Executive*. New York: New York University Press, 1984.

Jones, Charles O. "Congress and the Presidency." In *The New Congress*, pp. 223–49. Edited by Thomas Mann and Norman Ornstein. Washington: American Enterprise Institute, 1978.

————. "Keeping faith and losing Congress: The Carter experience in Washington." *Presidential Studies Quarterly* 14 (Summer 1984): 437–445.

————. "Presidential negotiations with Congress." In *Both Ends of the Avenue*, pp. 96–130. Edited by Anthony King. Washington: American Enterprise Institute, 1983.

Kayden, Xandra, and Eddie Mahe, Jr. *The Party Goes On*. New York: Basic Books, 1985.

Kearns, Doris. *Lyndon Johnson and the American Dream*. New York: Harper and Row, 1976

Kernell, Samuel. "Campaigning, governing, and the contemporary Presidency." In *The New Direction in American Politics*, pp. 117–41. Edited by John E. Chubb and Paul E. Peterson. Washington: Brookings Institution, 1985.

————. *Going Public: New Strategies of Presidential Leadership*. Washington: Congressional Quarterly Press, 1986.

————, and Samuel L. Popkin, editors. *Chief of Staff: Twenty-Five Years of Managing the Presidency*. Berkeley, CA: University of California Press, 1986.

Kessel, John. "The structures of the Carter White House." *American Journal of Political Science* 27 (August 1983): 431–63.

————. "The structures of the Reagan White House." *American Journal of Political Science* 28 (May 1984): 231–258.

King, Anthony. "A mile and a half is a long way." In *Both Ends of the Avenue*, pp. 246–73. Edited by Anthony King. Washington: American Enterprise Institute, 1983.

———, editor. *Both Ends of the Avenue*. Washington: American Enterprise Institute, 1983.

———, editor. *The New American Political System*. Washington: American Enterprise Institute, 1978.

Kraft, Joseph. "The post-imperial Presidency." New York *Times Magazine*, November 2, 1980, pp. 31–95.

Ladd, Everett Carl. "Alignment and realignment: Where are the voters going?" *The Ladd Report*, #3. New York: W. W. Norton, 1986.

Lambro, Donald. "What did the 1986 election tell us?" *The World & I* (January 1987): 104–107.

Leacacos, John P. "Kissinger's apparat." *Foreign Policy* 5 (Winter 1971): 3–27.

Leuchtenburg, William. *In the Shadow of FDR*. Ithaca, NY: Cornell University Press, 1983.

Light, Paul. *The President's Agenda*. Baltimore: Johns Hopkins University Press, 1982.

———. *Vice-Presidential Power*. Baltimore: Johns Hopkins University, 1984.

McDonald, Forrest. *The Presidency of George Washington*. Lawrence, KS: University Press of Kansas, 1974.

McMurty, Virginia. "OMB's role in the federal budget process." In *Office of Management and Budget: Evolving Roles and Future Issues*, pp. 1–72. Prepared by the Congressional Research Service, Library of Congress, Washington: Government Printing Office, 1986.

Meier, Kenneth J. *Regulation*. New York: St. Martin's Press, 1985.

Moe, Richard. "Taming the N.S.C." New York *Times*, November 26, 1986, p. 1.

Moe, Ronald C. "Central legislative clearance." In *Office of Management and Budget: Evolving Roles and Future Issues*, pp. 169–84. Washington: GPO, 1986.

Moe, Terry M. "The politicized Presidency." In *The New Direction in American Politics*, pp. 235–272. Edited by John E. Chubb and Paul E. Peterson. Washington: Brookings Institution, 1985.

Moynihan, Daniel Patrick. "The 'new Science of politics' and the old art of government." *The Public Interest* 86 (Winter 1987): 22–35.

Mulock, Bruce K. "Legislative vetoes and the independent regulatory agencies: Whose powers are being balanced and why?" *Congressional Research Service Review* (Fall 1983). Reprinted in U.S. House Committee on Rules. *Legislative Veto After Chadha*, pp. 204–8. Washington: Government Printing Office, 1984.

Nash, Bradley, et al. *Organizing and Staffing the Presidency*. New York: Center for the Study of the Presidency, 1980.

Nathan, Richard. *The Administrative Presidency*. New York: John Wiley, 1983.

Natoli, Marie D. *American Prince, American Pauper*. Westport, CT: Greenwood Press, 1985.

Neely, Richard. *How Courts Govern America*. New Haven, CT: Yale University Press, 1981.

Nelson, Michael. "Two steps forward (is) one step back: Post-Neustadtian presidential scholarship." *Presidency Research* 7 (Spring 1985): 22–27.

Neustadt, Richard. "Presidency and legislation: The growth of central clearance." *American Political Science Review* 48 (Summer 1954): 641–71.

———. *Presidential Power*, revised. New York: John Wiley, 1980.

Newland, Chester A. "Executive office policy apparatus: Enforcing the Reagan agenda." In *The Reagan Presidency and the Governing of America*, pp. 135–168. Edited by Lester M. Salamon and Michael S. Lund. Washington: Urban Institute Press, 1984.

Noll, Roger. *Reforming Regulation*. Washington: Brookings Institution, 1971.

Ornstein, Norman J. "Introduction." In *President and Congress: Assessing Reagan's First Year*, pp. 1–3. Edited by Norman J. Ornstein. Washington: American Enterprise Institute, 1982.

———. "The open Congress meets the president." In *Both Ends of the Avenue*, pp. 185–211. Edited by Anthony King. Washington: American Enterprise Institute, 1983.

Ostrom, Charles W., Jr., and Dennis M. Simon. "The President and public support: A strategic perspective." In *The Presidency and Public Policy Making*, pp. 50–70. Edited by George C. Edwards, III, Steven Shull, and Norman Thomas. Pittsburgh: University of Pittsburgh Press, 1985.

———. "Promise and performance: A dynamic model of Presidential popularity." *American Political Science Review* 79 (June 1985): 334–58.

Palmer, John L., and Elizabeth V. Sawhill, editors. *The Reagan Record*. Washington: Ballinger, 1984.

———. *The Reagan Experiment*. Washington: Urban Institute Press, 1982.

Patterson, James T. *Congressional Conservatism in the New Deal*. Lexington: University Press of Kentucky, 1967.

Peterson, Mark A. "Interest groups and the Reagan White House: For whom the door bell tolls." Paper presented to the American Political Science Association, Washington, D.C., 1986.

Peterson, Paul E. "The new politics of deficits." In *The New Direction in American Politics*, pp. 365–97. Edited by John E. Chubb and Paul E. Peterson. Washington: Brookings Institution, 1985.

Pious, Richard M. *The American Presidency*. New York: Basic Books, 1979.

Polsby, Nelson W. *Consequences of Party Reform*. New York: Oxford University Press, 1983.

———. "The Democratic nomination and the evolution of the party system." In *The American Elections of 1984*, pp. 36–65. Edited by Austin Ranney. An American Enterprise Institute Book. Durham, NC: Duke University Press, 1985.

———. "The institutionalization of the U.S. House of Representatives." *American Political Science Review* 62 (March 1968): 144–68.

———. "Some landmarks in modern Presidential–Congressional relations." In *Both Ends of the Avenue*, pp. 1–25. Edited by Anthony King. Washington: American Enterprise Institute, 1983.

Porter, Roger. *Presidential Decision-Making: The Economic Policy Board*. New York: Cambridge University Press, 1980.

Reagan, Michael. *The Managed Economy*. New York: Oxford University Press, 1963.

Reagan, Ronald, with Richard G. Hubler. *Where's the Rest of Me*? New York: Duell, Sloan, and Pearce, 1965.

Reedy, George. *The Twilight of the Presidency*. New York: New American Library, 1970.

Rieselbach, Leroy N. *Congressional Reform in the Seventies*. Morristown, NJ: General Learning Press, 1977.

Ripley, Randall B. "Power in the post-World War II Senate." In *Studies of Congress*, pp. 297–320. Edited by Glenn R. Parker. Washington: Congressional Quarterly Press, 1985.

———, and Grace Franklin. *Policy Implementation and Bureaucracy*, 2nd edition. Chicago: Dorsey Press, 1986.

Robinson, Michael J. "Where's the beef? Media and media elites in 1984." In *The American Elections of 1984*, pp. 166–202. Edited by Austin Ranney. Durham, NC: Duke University Press, 1985.

Rohde, David W., Norman J. Ornstein, and Robert L. Peabody. "Political change and legislative norms in the U.S. Senate, 1957–1974." In *Studies of Congress*, pp. 147–88. Edited by Glenn R. Parker. Washington: Congressional Quarterly Press, 1985.

Rosenberg, Morton. "Regulatory Management at OMB." *Office of Management and Budget: Evolving Roles and Future Issues*, pp. 185–234. Washington: GOP, 1986.

Rossiter, Clinton. *The American Presidency*, 2nd ed. New York: Time, Inc., 1963.

Rourke, Francis E. "The Presidency and the bureaucracy." In *The Presidency and the Political System*, pp. 339–62. Edited by Michael Nelson. Washington: Congressional Quarterly Press, 1984.

Safire, William. "The '88 campaign begins." New York *Times*, October 13, 1986, p. 19.

———. "Only a Bay of Pigs." New York *Times*, November 27, 1986, p. 27.

Salamon, Lester M., and Michael S. Lund, editors. *The Reagan Presidency and the Governing of America*. Washington: Urban Institute Press, 1984.

Schick, Allen. "How the budget was won and lost." In *President and Congress: Assessing Reagan's First Year*, pp. 14–43. Edited by Norman J. Ornstein. Washington: American Enterprise Institute, 1982.

———. "The budget as an instrument of Presidential policy." In *The Reagan Presidency and the Governing of America*, pp. 91–125. Edited by Lester M. Salamon and Michael S. Lund. Washington: Urban Institute Press, 1984.

———. *Congress and Money*. Washington: Urban Institute Press, 1980.

———. *Reconciliation and the Congressional Budget Process*. Washington: American Enterprise Institute, 1981.

Schlesinger, Arthur, Jr. *The Imperial Presidency*. New York: Popular Library, 1974.

———. "Why not question the Presidency?" New York *Times*, January 2, 1987, p. 25.

Seidman, Harold, and Robert Gilmour. *Politics, Position, and Power*, 4th ed. New York: Oxford University Press, 1986.

Smoller, Fred. "The Six O'Clock Presidency: Patterns of network news coverage of the Presidency." *Presidential Studies Quarterly*, 16 (Winter 1986): 31–49.

Sorauf, Frank J. *Party Politics in America*, 5th ed. Boston: Little, Brown, 1984.

Sperlich, Peter. "Bargaining and overload: An essay on *Presidential Power*." *The Presidency*, pp. 168–192. Edited by Aaron Wildavsky. Boston: Little, Brown, 1969.

Stein, Herbert. *The Fiscal Revolution in America*. Chicago: University of Chicago Press, 1969.

Thatch, Charles. *The Creation of the Presidency, 1775–1789*. Baltimore: Johns Hopkins University Press, 1969; orig. pub. 1923.

Tugwell, Rexford G. *The Enlargement of the Presidency*. Garden City, NY: Doubleday, 1960.

U.S. Congress. House. Committee on Rules. *Legislative Veto After Chadha*. Hearings before the Committee on Rules. 98th Cong., 2nd sess., 1984.

U.S. Congress. *Legislation on Foreign Relations Through 1983*, Vol. I. Washington: Government Printing Office, 1984.

U.S. Congress. Senate. Committee on the Budget. *Gramm-Rudman-Hollings and the Congressional Budget Process*. Committee Print. 99th Cong., 1st sess., December 1985.

U.S. Congress. Senate. Committee on Environment and Public Works. *Executive Branch Review on Environmental Regulations*. Hearings before a subcommittee of the Committee on Environment and Public Works. 96th Cong., 1st sess., 1979.

U.S. Congress. Senate. Committee on Environment and Public Works. *Office of Management and Budget Influence on Agency Regulations*. Committee Print. 99th Congress, 2nd session, 1986.

U.S. General Accounting Office. *A Glossary of Terms Used in the Federal Budget Process*, 3rd ed. PAD–81–27. Washington: GAO, 1981.

U.S. President. President's Commission on Administrative Management. *Administrative Management in the Government of the United States*. Washington: Government Printing Office, 1937.

U.S. President. President's Special Review Board. *Report*, February 25, 1987. Washington: Government Printing Office. [The "Tower Commission" report.]

Wander, W. Thomas, F. Ted Hebert, and Gary W. Copeland, eds. *Congressional Budgeting*. Baltimore: Johns Hopkins University Press, 1984.

Wayne, Stephen J. "Congressional liaison in the Reagan White House: A preliminary assessment of the first year." In *President and Congress: Assessing Reagan's First Year*, pp. 44–65. Edited by Norman J. Ornstein. Washington: American Enterprise Institute, 1982.

———. *The Legislative Presidency*. New York: Harper and Row, 1978.

Weaver, R. Kent. "Controlling entitlements." In *The New Direction in American Politics*, pp. 307–341. Edited by John E. Chubb and Paul E. Peterson. Washington: The Brookings Institution, 1985.

West, William F., and Joseph Cooper. "The rise of administrative clearance." In *The Presidency and Public Policy Making*, pp. 192–214. Edited by George C. Edwards III, Steven Shull, and Norman Thomas. Pittsburgh: University of Pittsburgh Press, 1985.

Wildavsky, Aaron. *The Politics of the Budgetary Process*, 4th ed. Boston: Little, Brown, 1984.

———. "Presidential succession and disability: Policy analysis for unique cases." In *The Presidency*, pp. 777–95. Edited by Aaron Wildavsky. Boston: Little, Brown, 1969.

———. "The two Presidencies." In *The Presidency*, pp. 230–243. Edited by Aaron Wildavsky. Boston: Little, Brown, 1969.

Wilson, James Q. "Does the separation of powers still work?" *The Public Interest* 86 (Winter 1987): 36–52.

———. *The Politics of Regulation*. New York: Basic Books, 1980.

———. "Realignment at the top, dealignment at the bottom." In *The American Elections of 1984*, pp. 297–311. Edited by Austin Ranney. Durham, NC: Duke University Press, 1985.

Wyden, Peter. *Bay of Pigs*. New York: Simon and Schuster, 1979.

Wyzomirski, Margaret Jane. "The de-institutionalization of Presidential staff agencies." *Public Administration Review* 42 (September/October 1982): 448–58.

Young, James Sterling. *The Washington Community, 1800–1828*. New York: Harcourt, Brace, and World, 1966.

Index

About the Author

RYAN J. BARILLEAUX is an assistant professor of political science at Miami University, Ohio. He was formerly on the faculty of the University of Texas at El Paso and an aide to Senator J. Bennett Johnston. He received a doctorate from the University of Texas in 1983, and is the author of *The President and Foreign Affairs* and a number of studies on the presidency and public affairs.